A Poetic Touch ~The Human Condition

A book of poetry
Written by S. G. Lee

SB

An imprint of Shillelagh Books
London, Ontario, Canada

Acknowledgments:
Sincere thanks to Jodi and Sydney, without your constant support and encouragement, this book would not be possible. You are the best friends a writer could have. I dedicate this book to my daughters, my son-in law and my husband; who have supported my writing endeavours with encouragement and love. Special thanks to my beloved mother in heaven, who taught me dreams, can come true with hard work, perseverance and patience.

Table of Contents

Preface:

I've always loved poetry and this poetry is definitely
unfiltered and untrained as it comes from my heart.
I hope you enjoy and embrace the feeling, thought,
and sometimes humour I put into it. .

~0~

Section 1 - The Human Condition:

Being Human

*L*ife unexpected,

Happy one minute,
Sad the next
Worried and blue, joyful, glad,
How it does vext,
To be all things at once,
Yet none,
We feel,
We see,
We do,
It's all the same,
Life unexpected,
Happy one minute,
Sad the next,
We are human.

~~O~~

Loving Hands

(I wrote this for those who have someone sick and dying)

I'm terminal, not contagious,
Do not shut your eyes,
And pretend I'm not here,
Touch me with loving hands,
Warm hearts filled with cheer,
Caress me with tales of memories,

Take me to places,
We love to be,
Take me for walks,
Even in a wheelchair,

Hold my hand,
Like you'll never let me go,
But when I'm gone,
Please move on,
To happiness and cheer,
Know though I'm always near,

I want you happy,
Even if it means,
That someone else is there,

To hold your hand,
And wear your wedding band,

Move on to warm smiles,
A tender touch,
And someone who loves you just as much,
Just once in a while think of me,

Remember me with smiles,
No weeping and don't be sad,
Be joyful of the time we had,
Look at the beauty in the world,
And remember me.

~0~

Not Handout but Human Kindness

Not handout but human kindness,
Do not turn away in blindness,
Do you see them begging standing on the median
on the street?
Do you see the battered clothes the holes in shoes
on feet?
Do you see them hoping for enough change to eat?
Or perhaps to get a drink in this heat or cold?
Do you turn your head in disgust?
Or do you think I have so much?

A place to rest and somewhere to cook and heat,
A roof over my head and food a plenty to eat,
Money can be tight, but if I can buy a coffee,
That money would help you see,
To feed that person I can see,
Struggling and homeless before me,

How can I turn my back when it makes me,
Cry to see that someone,
In such a rich country,

How is that done?
That they go thirsty or hungry,
I can't turn my back, even when others scoff,
And say I bet they live in a comfortable loft,

The genuine thank-you's,
As money is given, smiles ensue,
Convinces me of their want,
Whom I to judge their need,
For only by the grace of God go I.

~~O~.

Parental Advice

Show me some kindness,
Give me encouragement,
To let me succeed,
Forgive my transgressions,
And teach me the way,
To be a better person today,
Do not put yourself on a pedestal,
From which I can't climb,
But deliver a smile,
A helping hand to reach for,
Teach me gently, your way,
But let me be me,
Let me make mistakes,
So I can learn,
And be the best I can be.

~0~

Stopping Bulling Begins With You!

T each your children,
To guard their tongues,
Do not let them hurt with words,
Unkind and hurtful,
For words unfettered cut the glass,
Fragile souls shatter.

Souls beautiful and standing tall,
Starting to wither at the vine,
Until battered, bruised and broken,
They wonder why they exist,
If only to be tortured and feel alone,

Reach out to these square pegs,
Riches in society,
These sensitive souls,
Have much to teach us,

Do not allow them to feel alone,
So confused they take their lives,
Depriving society, family, friends,
Of their gentle ways,

Their goodness we cannot behold,
God bless our broken souls,
For not recognizing their worth,
Reach out to them,
Let them know friendship,
Can come their way,
Let kindness be the way.

~0~

Violence

A child watching,

Doors slamming,
Voices raised,
Things thrown,
Fists raised,
Lies shattered,
In a moment
Everything changed,
Life's joy stolen,
Can it be ever found again?

~0~

Sexism

Do you like my wiggle?
Or just like my jiggle?
Walking early down the street,
Hoping that we don't meet,
Because your whistles make me,
Uncomfortable and you don't see,
That what you're doing,
Is disgusting,
I should be suing,
As it makes me cringe,
And twist inside
As I cry,
For I should feel like quality,
Even as I sigh,
Not some piece of meat,
I will not let you defeat,
All that I've done to make me,
Brand new,
Alive, and feeling free,
Will not be stolen,
By your taunts,
I will not be deterred,
From your haunts,
Just let me be!
~0~

Words Unspoken

Words unspoken,

Because we are afraid,
Time stands still,
As we try to get them out,
But by the time has long gone,
As we shout,
We don't speak up,
And people grow afraid,
The bullies take charge,
They have it made,
They can threaten,
And harm without fear,
Ignorance takes root,
It grows tall and wide,
For no one speaks,
And everyone complies,
With beliefs that harm,
And twist and grow,
Warping young minds,
And their souls,
As their mouths,
And actions harm,
Making their victims,
Want to cry,
Making their victims,
Want to die,

They have to stop,
They have to be taught,
From infancy to care,
For others as themselves,
To feel others pain,
That difference is good,
That no one is better,
Than anyone else,
That kindness is the fruit of life,
If it flows freely.
It flows gently back,
It makes the world
A better place,
For all to live and let live.

~0~

Empty Words

W ords seemingly empty words,
Sometimes for the birds,
As people speak,
The words they seek,

To comfort or to harm,
To seek or to alarm,
The two sides of every word,
Isn't it truly absurd?

How the same word can be,
Alarming or enlightening,
It can be truly frightening,
Or charming and sweet,
Sending out such heat,

Words choose them wisely,
Be somewhat miserly,
Don't seek to harm,
To hurt and alarm,

Be kind, be sweet,
Though it's no easy feat,
And you'll find words of yours,
Do not harm, do not cause wars,

Words used entirely for good,
May still be misunderstood,
But knowledge that you share,
May make the words less rare,

The kindness that you expound and speak,
Will give you the peace you seek,
Will come back to you tenfold,
So go use kindness be bold.,
Make kindness and good deeds reign,

~O~

Harm

Are you sure this is the one?

The weakest one you find?
That the barbs of words?
Will burrow and twist?
Deep inside the soul?
That should be the motto,
Of those who use words,
Weapons in their armoury,
But most don't think,
About the things they say,

They say that words don't hurt,
But we know that for deceit,
For words can charm,
The loneliest person,
Make their day,
But they also destroy,
With swift arrows,
Hitting targets,
Tunneling inside,
The heart,
And memories,

Forever waiting,
To be pulled out,
Analysed,
Mulled over,
The victim wondering,
What they did wrong,
Causing further harm,
Each and every day,
As the perpetrator carries on.

~O~

Venom

W ords can be beautiful,

Spreading joy and love,
Then there are the others,
Barbed wire twisting deep,
They find their prey,
Easily, burrowing down,
Twisting the stomach,
Of their victim,

With bite and venom,
They fester and surround,
The mind and the heart hurt,

Perpetrators confronted claim,
It was all a joke,
Attach no blame,
You're too sensitive,
They accuse,
Grow a thicker skin,
This isn't a world,
The victims want to live in,

Peace and harmony,
Is their troth,
Not chaos and strife,
How to come to terms?
Why should they be so tormented?

They become introverts,
Facing down the barbs,
By hiding in the shadows,
Away from harm.

~0~

Kindness

Life has twists and turns,
A chosen road not found,
Because when you choose the road to follow,
It weaves into a bump ahead a road unknown,

A place where everything changes,
Where down is up and up is down,
Where life leads you you'll never know,
So hold on tight and hold on tough,

Live, love life, and learn enough,
That you can really make a mark,
Of compassion and tolerance there's never given
enough,
So give as much as you can and remember its only
stuff,

You can help others if you only try,
A simple smile, a winsome grin,
Can make someone's day just a little better,
But a dollar you can readily spare,
Makes someone's life change.

~O~

Let' s

W e often say,

Let's do this,
Let's change our ways,
But do we really?
Alter our behaviour?
Let's do this instead,
Let's be kinder,
Let's be more compassionate,
Let's find the bright side of things,
Let's smile a little more,
And complain a little less,
Let's give a helping hand,
When one is needed,
Without being asked,
Let's be there,
When someone cries,
Not to judge but to,
Offer a shoulder,
Let's show our gentleness,
As proudly as we can,
Let's touch people with our hearts,
For life is short,
And full of trials,
Let's be better people,
We can only try,
So the world can be,
A better place,
Let's!

Feisty

Being feisty is a not a curse,

But a trait that gets you through,
Life's trials and tribulations,
When meddlesome curves come your way,
You go with the flow and try a method,
To find your path once again,
Taking a stab at living,
Life on your terms,
At finding money,
As well as love again,
When unhappiness comes your way,
You look for that shiny sun, beneath the cloud,
Till the sun comes out again,
And you feel the warmth again.

~0~

Presence

A presence,

Unknown,
Unseen,
A black hole,
Of non-existence,
I am forgotten.

To live out,
My life in,
Obscurity,
I sit, I wait,
In shadow,

I creep to,
The light,
Seen all,
At once,
Shining bright,
I am known,
But for how long?

~0~

Change

The wind says change and yet there I go,
Although I don't like to go with the flow,
Change comes hard, I like my space,
Having everything in just one place,
But time marches on and nothing stays,
No matter how and whine and flay,
I must move on and be the best I can be,
Look around and truly see,
What change can mean to all of us,
Quit moaning and making a fuss,
Everything changes so I can't stay still,
Of everything, I must take my fill,
Enjoy my time and place,
Enjoy the things in my space,
Remembering with change emanates beauty ever
after,
And yes maybe if I'm lucky, a little laughter,
Some joy, some sadness, it's true,
But lots of things to see and do,
Life has its twists its turns you see,
But we can all make the best of it and be,
Happy if we choose.

~O~

To Dream Again

I dreamed a dream unfilled,

Of beauty to behold,
Of life and love and happiness,
I faltered and fell,
I cried,
I awoke to a life,
And dared to dream again,
To find my life's dream fulfilled.

~0~

Live and Let Live

I turn on the news and wonder why,

People seem to be so much crazier,
Are they so bogged down with life?
That they do not care about anyone?
Or anything that shares their space?
So trodden down that they do such awful things,
That make me shout and that make others cry,
Are their feelings numb and withered?
Is there ice water in their veins?

What makes someone want to harm another?
People point fingers at television and video games,
There must be someone or something to blame,
Is it really mental illness unchecked, that fuels,
These flames of violence and harm?

Or is it society's views and statements without
thinking,
Of violence and harm, pictures can do no harm,
They say gun sighted targets don't incite,
And yet people see and it engrains,
On brains of undeveloped minds,
That threatening people is okay,

I do not know the answer I wish I did,
I wish I knew how to stop this river of violence,
That seems to fill the hearts of people,
Young and old, but love is stronger than hate,
Have opinions, but don't incite hatred,
Reach out and do good,
So practice kindness and forgive,
And make the world a better place,
For all to live and let live.

~0~

The Book of Life

T hunder rumbles and rages,

As we turn the pages,
Like in a favorite book,

As we see the path we took,
When do we say,
We've seized the day?
Enough it's truly enough!
Why do we hold onto this stuff?

We have a past,
Like all it doesn't last,
We move on we seek the peace we haven't known,
And like a warm comfy blanket,

We seek unfurled and sewn,

It covers us with warmth and comfort,
We find this warm feeling,
This person so appealing,
They are like a piece of you,
What can you say or do?

You surrender to the light,
Without a single fight,
The sun shines and we are happy,

The love that's kind of sappy,
Though tough times come,
And yes, bury some,
You cling to your single hope,
Sometimes you feel like a dope!
But then you realize,
Like someone who is suddenly wise,
How lucky you really are,
You've come so very far,
Life isn't perfect or even quite fair,
Sometimes it even strips you bare,
But the life you lead the people you touch,
Of all things this means so very much,
Because when you're gone and you are dust,
Will someone cry and make a fuss?
Will they think you made a difference in their life?
That you made it easier they have less strife?

Will you be remembered in the pages of a life?
A mother, a husband, a father a child a wife?
Will you have achieved a goal or helped someone?
Made a difference and brought them the sun?

A warm smile, an open heart,
Strangers never when you part,
The pages of the book,
Written in the memories and minds,
Of the people you touch,
The love, the ties that truly bind,

These things define the life you lead,
You're every thought, you're every deed,
Though you struggle and have some strife,
For the pages are written in your book of life.

~0~

Beauty

Peeople search faces for beauty,
True beauty shines in the eyes,
For within is the soul,
From which all beauty flows.

~0~

Smile and Make the World Go Round

Love laughter and joy,
Are not just for a ploy,
Sweet words uttered,
As peace fluttered,
People's happy joyful lives,

It only takes a smile,
A kind word does beguile,
The senses with its simplicity,
As it spreads through every ethnicity,
Peace reigns supreme,

But that is just a dream,
For in some hearts,
Is the need to needle and sin,
Harm all that is good,
Turning those who to would,
Follow their evil darkness,

Only those who think before,
They speak even the score,
For those single lights,
Keep the world's brights,
Burning brilliantly and make peace reign,

Smile like there is no tomorrow,
Grin like there is no sorrow,
Reach out a hand and help those who need,
For your reward, smiles and a happy heart.
Love makes the world go round.

~0~

Rose Coloured Glasses

Our eyes wide open yet we can't see,

The evil that lurks and hides,
We choose to not see,
I'd know I'd rather see,
The world through rosy coloured glasses,

We want to think that people are good,
And kind and sweet, yet sometimes,
We see the evil that lurks and hides,
As it comes out from under its rock,

How it lingers on the edge of our vision,
As we grasp it's shape and shut it down,
With words and actions,

Our world is a place of peace and calm,

Yet again as new, but is it really?

Or do we have our heads in the sand,
Pretending believing all is well,
When evil lives on hiding,
Waiting for the opportunity,
To come out and play again.

~0~

Life

Life is a golden chain,

With twists and turns,
Sometimes frayed,
But the links can always be fixed,
Made better,
To let it shine again.

~0~

Lighting Your Inner Light

Light your inner light,
With kindness so bright,
With sweet intentions,
Of great inventions,
Of giving without reward,
Well smiles you look forward,
In your blossoming sight,
To seeing that light,
Take away all that annoy,
Making the world peace and joy,
Your soul reward.

~0~

Ever Thankful

Growing old is a privilege,

These wrinkles I do not hide,
For each one I've gained,
Life's lesson I've learned,
Experience I have added,
Time I have spent
Others have been denied.

How could I wish them away,
Moments spent in wonder and joy,
Sorrow and sadness,
Life's journey cannot be denied,
Each minute is a blessing,
To spend time with loved ones,

So as the seasons change and sand,
Trickles through the hourglass,
I thank God,
For the wrinkles I sport,
And the gray hair coming through,
For I have been granted new life,
Each day I awake,
And I am ever thankful still.

~0~

River of Life

Life is a river flowing,

In all its might and glory,
Occasionally the current is swift,
Other times it flows,
Like a babbling brook,

But always it challenges,
Leaves one wet and cold one minute,
Warm and toasty the next,
Sometimes we bounce,
Floating above the fray,
Other times we sink,
So low we cannot rise,

And others lift us up,
Humans are resilient,
Buoyant in design,
The river of life,
Gives as much as it takes,
As we soldier on,
This path we call life,
The river continues on.
~0~

Self-Absorbed

Are we self-absorbed,

Thinking we feel deeply,
About issues of nature,
And the turning tide,
As we ignore,
The weather changes,
Those signifying,
Earth fighting back,
Against us,
Its parasites,
While we drift along,
Living life,
Never speaking out,
Shouldn't we be frantic?

Waiting for the other shoe to fall?
But instead we hide our heads,
Within our shells,
Hoping to be rescued,
In the end.
~0~

The Privilege is Mine

Misery likes company, they say,

But I like to chase misery away,
Stale dreams must be put aside,
Dreams are but wispy cobwebs,
Easily brushed away,
While new ones are made,

We cannot always have what we want,
But we can dream of the future,
We want and can obtain,
Small things, turned into big ones,
Even if life and fate turns on a dime,

We can find happiness,
If we try closing our eyes and wishing,
The privilege of living each day,
When others are rebuffed,
No more days for them,

Is a hard cross to bear,
But we soldier on,
Making the best of the time,
We have been granted,

Creating a better world,
Even if only in our small space,
To be proud of,

A legacy, if only to family,
Of good things done,
Let the other deeds,
Be unsung, unrenowned,
But always remarkable.

~0~

Soar

,,.•*¨¨*• ♫♪ ♪♫ •*¨¨*•.,,,,.•*¨¨*• ♫♪♫♪ ♪♫.•*

T he music ripples over me,

Clean ripping back the fleshy layers,
That bind my soul keeping it prisoner,
Music pierces the brain and the heart,
And I soar like a bird,

,,.•*¨¨*• ♫♪ ♪♫ •*¨¨*•.,,,,.•*¨¨*• ♫♪♫♪ ♪♫.•*

Happiness within and without me,
As my voice sings along,
Exhilaration, delight and bliss,
Are mine to share,
I am free this earthly bonds,
If only for the length of a song.
,,.•*¨¨*• ♫♪ ♪♫ •*¨¨*•.,,,,.•*¨¨*• ♫♪♫♪ ♪♫.•*¨

~0~

Life' s Essence

Y ou gave your blood,

Your life's essence,
To save my life,
Without it,
I would have crippled,
And died,

My bodies' defenses weak,
The bacteria lurking,
My need great,
You didn't know me,
You didn't know my need,

But you came to,
Heed the call,
The blood banks cry,
When the need was greatest,

No fee given just cookies,
And thanks,
The greatest one you'll ever get,

You'll never know,
Is the gratitude from me,
For my life extended,
Thank-you.

~0~

Adventure

Life is the adventure,
Ups downs and in-betweens,
It takes us on a journey,

We can't truly understand,
Until we complete it,
And complete it we must,
The moments that make us weep,
The ones that makes us smile,
The joy that people can give,
And then take away,

A circle of endless beginnings,
And saddening ends,
The things we then learn,
How else would we know?
All that we need to know?
And find our own place in the universe?

~0~

Love thy Fellow Man

If I were you and you were me,

What colour would the sky be?
The differences in psychological thinking,
Are plain to see,
No impulsiveness for,
Them to worry about as,
Some fear for themselves,
Not their fellow man,

Creed, colour, or sexual orientation,
Each made in God's image,
Nothing too sparse,
For them to become morose,
Just advice plain and simple,
To love your fellow man,

Stand up against injustice,
Stand up when it's hard,
Stand and be counted,
Treat each other with kindness,
Love thy fellow man.

~0~

Relevant

People can be too liberal,

Be too quarrelsome,
They want to be profane,
Because they can hide behind,
Anonymity, no face,
No address for them,
They can be anything,
They want to be,
Who could know?
That they're not media,
When they claim to be,
People believe what they read,
They have presence they are relevant,
In the moment,
But sooner or later,
People move on from what's popular,
And find the next best thing.

~0~

Happy

Older people, seniors they are called,
Living out their lives in,
A dreary retirement village,
What a farce?
They're kicking up their heels,
Camaraderie here, the smiles glistening,
On their faces as they feel lucky,
To participate in a video,
To show how happy they are,
They are joyful in the moment,
Activities make them content,
But visitors, especially family,
Make them sing this song for real,
Make it happen,
Visit older family today.

~0~

For my grandmother who was always there for me and smiled when I visited
her once a week.

Section 2 - Reading, Writing and Encouragement:

Joy of Song

,,.•*¨¨*• ♫♪ ♪♫ •*¨¨*•.,,,,.•*¨¨*• ♫♪

I peer behind the curtain and I see,

All the world looking back at me,
The insecurity I feel my stomach hurting,
If only I could be more asserting,

,,.•*¨¨*• ♫♪ ♪♫ •*¨¨*•.,,,,.•*¨¨*• ♫♪

I hear the whispers note the smiles,
And yet it's the silence that riles,
I take a breath and open my mouth to sing,
The world disappears as the notes ring,
,,.•*¨¨*• ♫♪ ♪♫ •*¨¨*•.,,,,.•*¨¨*• ♫♪

My spirit soars all the world is away,
The light in me glows like a ray,

,,•*"*• ♫♪♪♫ •*"*•.,,,,•*"*• ♫♪

,,•*"*• ♫♪ ♪♫ •*"*•.,,,,•*"*• ♫♪

The gift of song is mine in hand,
As the notes come out without a band,
I sing, I dance, under the lights,
As the spirits take flights,
And as the song ends,
It's as if it mends,
The person who hides inside,

,,•*"*• ♫♪ ♪♫ •*"*•.,,,,•*"*• ♫♪

In the music I can confide,
My hopes my dreams my ever after,
Without the inner laughter,
I feel the joy the peace within,
And wonder if it's a sin?
To hide in the music?
But feel all within?

,,•*"*• ♫♪ ♪♫ •*"*•.,,,,•*"*• ♫♪

~0~

New Books

New books the crispy clean feel,

As you hold it in your hands,
As the story inside appeals,
And takes you to distant lands,
The words that are there are black and bold,
Weaving stories of danger and love and lust,
In your hands the stories, twist and turns unfold,
Your continued, grave attention a given must,

Books!

I love the feel in my hands,
The smell from musty to crisp and new,
As the pages turn and expand,
My need to own and to share with you,

Books!

The stories that I've read,
Of truth and adventure,
Lying prone in my bed,
Stories of true censor,
Weaving stories of danger and love and lust,
In your hands the stories,
Twist and turns unfold,
Your continued, grave attention a given must,

Books!

I love the feel in my hands,

The smell from musty to crisp and new,
As the pages turn and expand,
My need to own and to share with you,
The stories that I've read,
Of truth and adventure,
Lying prone in my bed,
Stories of true censor,

Books!

Books I love to have,
And re-read again,
A type of salve,
For my soul to send,
Me soaring, my imagination,
Unfurled, unburdened fun,

Books!

How I love them,
~0~

Reading

O pening a book is,

Like streak of beauty in the night,
As the notion takes flight,
Of sitting down,
To dream of worlds unknown,
Reading of feelings grown,
Of wars lost and won,
Of life's struggles and dreams,
Nothing can be read,
That cannot be seen,

In the mind's eye it gleams,
And when we pick up a book,
It goes on and on,
Till we reach the end,
And set it down again.

~0~

Writers

Writers have a need to express,

The inner stories locked inside,
Sharing imagination and emotions,
They've wrought through characters,
They've grown to love,
As if they're real,
Through careful observation of life lived,
Of pain felt and joys obtained,
They write of life and love and death,

Writers need community,
Of which they sup,
Promoting and wooing,
Each other's work,
Giving birth to ideas,
Stories and poems,
Filling minds with ideas,
Expanding and enlightening,
Minds young and old,

Writer's feelings are expressed,
Shared with readers one and all,
Calloused fingers are their reward,
The written page our oxygen,
To live on and on.
~0~

Addiction

A dream, a wish at my fingertips,

A whisper in my mind,
A story takes root fresh from my lips,
To the paper and computer it binds,
A need, an addiction that takes flight,
A tentative need to see the light,

Of words and emotions and stories fulfilled,
Of all the things to see and build,
Of things to amuse and titillate,
Of people, places, and things to relate,
Of situations unforetold,

Of people, oh so bold,
Fill my computer and my mind,
The pictures that design,
Weaving stories for people to enjoy,

Maybe to slightly annoy,
Because the addiction calls me near,
And makes me write the stories so dear,
To my heart and mind,
Something others want to find,
And read and read,
That is my need.

~0~

Tell the Tale

I feel the words begin to flow,

I tell them, *"Please do not go."*
The story continues to fill my computer,
And then slowly it begins to peter,

I ponder staring out at the birds,
Pacing to and fro where are the words?
I stare at the screen blank and blinking,
What in the world was I thinking?
I can't write how could I, I'm not a writer,
I think and how can I make this story tighter,
And then it begins the words flow,
And I found out what I'd always know,

I am a writer with stories to tell,
And it's not just about the sell,
But about sharing the tales,
That calls me and hails,
Screaming within me,
TELL THE TALE!

~O~

Write to Flight

I put words fit to flight,
Of eagles soar and fright,
And then with someone's might,
Their computer they write,
Of dreams wiped away,
Of people not what I'd say,
Destroying the dreams in me,
As my compulsion does flee,

I look I see it lying in a flash,
My writing thrown to the trash,
Destroyed by their typing and sad twisted
comments,
Their need to control their need to control events,
Their need to be the only one standing,
As my dream I am abandoning,
To try and find a new one,
With a click and a nod I'm done,

I am where words soar and light,
It's there with no more fight,
No more with an invisible foe,
Who sits and preens and smiles,
But it does bring up my bile,
For they think they have won,

But internet gives them freedom,
They think to do what they will,
And so they find a new victim,
To terrorize at will.

~0~

Alive and Well

*I wrote this more than five years ago impatient for things to change
obviously things have changed since then but I thought you might
enjoy this poem anyway.*

T he mistletoe that makes me itch,

The ginger that gives me hives,
And closes my throat,
Making it hard to breathe,
The lights, which shine making me look,

Older than time itself,
The music that plays,

,,.•*¨*• ♫♪ ♪♫ •*¨*•.,,,,.•*¨*• ♫♪
Making me sad,
Telling me I'm a year older,
And what have I done?
But sitting at my computer typing,
The words that keeps my story,
Alive and well,
As I wait for that agent or publisher,
To see just what I see in me,
A published writer,
The world to see,
As they read my book,
And enjoy the stories,
I have wrought from my mind,
Of murder and mayhem,
And families true,
Of love and laughter,
And happiness too,

I just know that this year,
To come, so new,
Will be the year too,
For all my dreams come true.

~0~

Believe

This is for those who need to be inspired and believe in themselves

B elieve, writers storytellers all,
Believe in yourself,
You must trust,
That belief can bring you so very much,
Believe!
You have a gift that creates a world,
That tells a story all unfurled,
Of life and love and loss,
Believe!
Don't let those words gather moss,
Trust that you can make,
Your readers sit up and take,
Notice of your talent and prose,
Believe!
As the words, they simply
flow.
Believe!
~0~

Feeding the Muse

Writing and writing some more,
Stressing and fretting myself,
Keeping up with and feeding my muse,
Wanting to write so much it really hurts,
Having the words stuck in my head,

Long years of neglect pouring out,
As the words get out and breathe,
Giving life to stories and poems,
Giving life to characters who wanted,
To see the light and to really be seen,

By others as they read and see,
And maybe like the characters,
And want to read more of the stories,
The poems that are stick in the recesses,
Of my mind that touch my soul,

Slow down says my body,
There is lots of time of mine to share,
The illusions, the poems, and stories,
Years to share and readers to please,
And pleasure to share, what is mine,

But a little voice says hurry up,
Get it done time is shorter than you know,
So I type my computer lets the words out,
And I write the words and finish the story,
And start reading it over and writing more,
Again the muse has won,
It's feeding begins anew.
~0~

Imaginations, Lost and Found

T he world is whirling round and round,

As snow goes falling to the ground,
My heart beats faster my fingers turn cold,
As I build a snowman as the story told,

A hat of black on his head, a pipe of clay,
A carrot for the nose, a right of play,
I cannot find but who cares,
Stones for buttons down its chest,
I wait I stare and bide my time,

Waiting for the snowman sublime,
But the snowman just starts to melt,

He doesn't come alive, a blow is dealt,
I must stop my imagining and act my age,
Not ten anymore but eleven with older sage,
Knowing magic doesn't exist I start to wonder why,
Do you have to put away childhood imaginings,
why?

It's fun to have a snowman that comes alive,
A pool of snow is made of which to dive,
A fort that built for pirates of snow,
Why, oh why, does our imagination have to go?
I decide it never has to go,

I'll keep my imagination burning,
In books and stories I am yearning,
To read and write,
And tell of fight,
Of battles played,
And things forbade,
I'll tell the tales forever more,
And let my imagination soar.

~0~

Dreaming Big and Bold

I dreamed of skyscrapers,

Heights to scales,
I dreamed of life untold,
Of dreaming big,
And dreaming bold,

But one day I put aside my dreams,
Life had taken out all my steam,
I promised myself it wasn't forever,
Just for now it wasn't never,

I would find my place,
And my own space,
To dream again of skyscrapers,
And heights to scale,
Life wouldn't beat me,
Down and crumble,
I'd pick myself up,
And go on,

And now I'm seeking those dreams,
Again those things that were just gleams,
Of ideas in my head,
I will not seek defeat,
I'll succeed because I know,

I can, I really can,
For all those things I struggled through,
And all the things I've done,
Have made me more,
Determined to be,
Who I am!

~0~

Section 3 ~ What a Writer Does

Everything is Still Possible

A single stream, a babbling brook,

A breeze blowing through
The cobblestones of my notice,
Blowing out the cobwebs,
The bad memories, the broken dreams,
I left in the subconscious of my mind,

Making room for new imaginings,
New visions, new people to love,
Aspirations unfulfilled, realities to face,
Everything moved away into its proper place,

But still within me the child dwells,
Who asks and whines,
Who dreams of heights difficult to climb?
But striving to achieve my dreams I've stilled,
I find the inner child,
Who knows everything is still possible.
~0~

Achieve

Dreams once dead in the water,

Hungry for new born ones,
As self-doubt threatens,
To extinguish the flame,
Nagging uncertainty,
Almost bringing me to my knees,
Little voices shouting
Fake, charlatan, phoney!
Weak, imitation, pretender!

A new voice says,
Ignore the dissent,
Be bold, be brave,
Dream big and achieve,
Your secret aspirations,
Hard work can attain all.

~0~

Possibilities

Possibilities, career dreams,

Should not be dashed,
By insipid small minded,
Petty, jealous, sexist creatures,
Who seek to end competition,
By snide comments,
Demoralizing and stealing,
Away confidence in one's abilities,
Sometimes when one is young,
One needs a little voice that says,
I am worthy,
I am important,
I am smart,
I am confident,
I am competent,
Instead of the manipulative people,
Who wait in the wings,
To fill that empty space,
With indecisiveness and your self-loath,
Then benefit from their scheming,
Taking not their rightful place,
Laughing at the discomfort,
That they have havocked,
Instead take the reins believe,
That you can achieve,
Whatever you set your heart,
And mind to
You are stronger than you think.

Filling the Soul

I have heard the call,

I have seen the light,
Of infinite goodness,
To share human kindness,
To share a smile,
To share a word,
To make someone's load lighter,
Is the ultimate goal,
Of all to fill the soul,
With the light that shimmers,
As it is passed on from person,
To person in simple acts,
Of kindness.

~0~

Section 4 - Family

Home

A dream,
A wish,
Home,
A need,
That passes,
On by,
No permanence,
And then is found,
Through work,
And strife,
At last,

A bounty of fish,
A humble apple pie,

A kitchen gleaming,
Cabinets surround,
A woman screaming,
In unsurpassed joy,
Her love is found,

A home and hearth,
To make her life,
A place to have rebirth,
To be someone's wife,
To open that door,
And step on through,
To walk the floor,
With babes in arms,
To grow old,
Hand in hand,
To have someone,
To understand,
Life's challenges,
Are taken in stride,
With a partner,
At your side.

~0~

My Child

It wasn't so long ago, I held you in my hands,

Took you to the beach to feel the sand,
Watched you take your first little steps to walk,
And then as you began to talk and talk,

I watched you biting my nails as you went to
school,
I watched you smiling, as you learned to swim a
pool,
Challenged the school to do better when bullies
bothered you,
Watched you grow into a person to admire as the
time it flew,

Encouraged you to go to school, to university,
To learn and grow all you could,
Watched you become the adult I knew you to be,
Doing everything you should,

I couldn't be more proud as a parent,
And it could be more apparent,
That you are grown and need me less,
To come in and pick up the mess,
Or tell you what to do,
Oh how the time it flew,
But now that you older and have grown,
It's time to let go,
Your life is waiting all the seeds I have sown,
Have blossomed and so,

It's time to let go,

You need to be on your own,
I will pick up the phone,
Calling you once in awhile,
As you live your life my once little child,

It's not goodbye, just letting go,
For you are my child,
Forever and please know,
I am and always will be your biggest fan,
I know you will go far, because you can.

~0~

Always

I can't go with you,

I don't know how,
You can smuggle me in your case,
I know you're laughing,
For it is written on your face,

But with all the Christmas,
You're taking home,
It fills your bag and purse,
There's no more room,
For me,

What, you think I'm not serious?
That I wouldn't go with you?
I'd go in a heartbeat,
By plane, by train, by boat,
But you have your life now,
And you need your space,

We'll talk face to face,
I'll see you next year,
My darling daughter,
You'll be here always,
Within my heart,

A call away,
If you need me,
I'll always be there,
No distance too great,
No distance to far,
For I am your mother,
Always!

~0~

Passing on the Pack Rat Gene

Busy running to and fro,
Packing everything as I go,
Wondering what to give away,
What I think must really stay,
Where will I put all this stuff?
Maybe there is just too much?
So back I go to start again,
I begin to put aside to send,
To charity and then,
My daughter says keep it all,
But the pile is too tall,
Oh dear, my fault?
She has the gene,
I cannot halt,
Just because she thinks,
She may need it again.

~0~

A Window to the Past

Looking at the photograph,

Its edges yellowed and brown,
A window to the past,
Taken when moving fast,
A picture from the bygone years,
Who thought it would last,
A blip in time
Isn't it sublime?

A little boy, a child so sweet,
Barely toddling on his little feet,
Captured for all time and space,
Climbing on a chair,
A devilish face,
Yet so sweet,
He seems to walk off the print,
Can he really give you a hint?
Of who he was and where he's been?

~0~

Mother

A mother loves you forever,

She's there in spirit,
Even when she's gone,
She's there!
Her words reverberate,
Of wisdom and love,
Echoing in your head,

You look at your face,
As you age and see,
Her there, and smile,
To see you share,
The magnificence,
That was your mother,
Of the beauty of her soul,
And the love she left behind,

You think of her and,
Thank God for time spent,
With her and for the loan,
He gave you of an angel,
From above, to take you,
In her arms, shelter you from storm,
And teach you how to stand alone,
When all she can give you is a feeling,
That she's beside you, to guide you still,

And know her love can see you through,
For as long as you think of her,
Dream of her,
Remember,
She lives,
In memory,
Thoughts,
And deeds,
She lives,
Forever.

~0~

Dad

Dad you taught me so many things,

True generosity of spirit,
And what that can really bring,
To enrich one's life,

You taught me loving someone means,
You put them first even when not seen,
As you struggled with your own battles,
Of ill health, troubled times and fate's rattles,
You put us first in your thoughts and mind,
We always knew of your love like a neon sign,

You taught me of history,
Of how much of life that's a mystery,
Of how adversity makes you stronger,
Whining makes things stay bad longer,

You taught me to appreciate nature,
Flowers so blue,
And castles in the sand,
You taught me just by watching you,
How to fix things on demand,

I miss you very much Dad,
And sometimes it makes me sad,
Not to have you here,

Someone who I love so dear,
But when I see beautiful rows of many flowers,
I think of you and know God in his infinite powers,
Has you tending his gardens keeping them in rows,
As sure as I know the wind blows,
I know you watch over me,

Always near, though I don't see,
Your love lives on,
As my life goes on,
Someday I will see,
You again,
Dad.
~0~

Whispered Words of Wisdom

W hispered words of wisdom,

Flow through me every day,
As I hear your voice still,
Father dear, still close to me,

Like little echoes from the past,
They tell me that you love me,
Tell me I'm your little girl,

Tell me that I'll go far in life,
That you're proud of me still,

I hear your epic tales,
Of battles on distant shores,
Of history brought to life,
Within your words,

I hear your romantic stories,
Of true love come to life,
And how lucky you were,
To make my mother for your wife,

I remember your goofy smile,
That told me how much you cared,
How you loved your children,
More than your life itself,

You were the best of fathers,
You loved, you lived,
You sacrificed and gave,
So your children could do well,

I know you are well and happy,
Looking on us all from above,
Know that your children love,
And miss your loving council still.

~0~

Love of Yarns

Dad you gave me a love of yarns,
Stories of history too,
Fairies and leprechauns filled your fables,
Music told some stories,
Records of bagpipes too,

A love for home and family,
A gentleness shown to all alike,
To animals kindness too,
Loving in all your actions,
Family came before your needs,
It showed in all your caring deeds

You weren't perfect, who could be?
But you were the best Father you could be,
I was happy to be, Daddy's little girl,
One of four girls, two boys, his children,
He loved so well.

You worried about your children,
Their safety and their lives, for you to lend.
A few more days to worry and contend,
That they would be okay without you,
You made plans of what we could do,
Even though you're gone to your heavenly reward,
Always know you are adored,
I thank God,
That I am always
Daddy's little girl.

~0~

My Little Girl

My little girl,
You held my heart,
In your little palms,
From the start,
Your gentle way,
The things,
You thought to say,
Made me smile,
For you did beguile,
All around you,
My bundle of joy,

You have a wit,
A gift for English lit,
A tremendous questioning brain,
That would interrogate the rain,
That seeks to learn,
And even discern,
The secrets of the ancient,
You seek to hunt,
For information,
That fills books,

S. G. Lee

You charm,
And disarm,
Dissenters,
I am so proud of you,

All the events you do,
The things you've accomplished,
How you've found your niche,
Make me burst with pride,
Even though you've grown,
May you always be my little girl!

~0~

Daddy

T hat lopsided grin,

Melts my heart,
The slight blemish,
On your cheek,
Signifies your youth,
How I adore you,
As you sit up so erect,
Holding me in your arms,
Daddy.

~0~

Little Brother

L ittle brother,

I remember those carefree days,
When we were young,
And played the days away,
Wooden swords and soldier men,
Parachutes and G.I. Joe,
Swinging on swings,
Running to and fro,
Wondering aimlessly through fields,
Forests and high ground,
Building sandcastles in the sand,
Swimming in the ocean holding logs,
Floating and kicking our legs,
Learning how to swim,
You were Batman,
To my Robin,
Inseparable.
I threatened the bullies,
Who took advantage of your size,
With my book bags,
I swung,

And away they would run,
My little brother, not always near now,
But always dear in my heart,
Memories of our childhood,
Always keep you there.
~0~

Feral

Her appetite insatiable,

She shred the meat,
With her tiny pointed teeth,
Her pale pink tongue,
Darting in and out,
Then she fled under the sofa,
To hid some more,
Her paw comes out,
Swish, swish goes her tail,
How she loves to hide,
My beloved cat Tina.

~0~

Old Loves New Loves

The bride stood with heart filled,

The groom beamed his heart healed,
The vows they said to cherish each other,
Not forgetting moving forward, loving one another,
Seeing the good and the bad,
Letting go of the nausea that set in,
To living and loving someone else; letting new life
begin,
Never forgetting the loves past gone on,
Just realizing they are not here,
They are left to live on,
They say their vows no fear,
A party began with all their loved ones dear,

To celebrate,
An all to elevate,
Their love for the couple,
Old, yet now so new.

~0~
(For Bonnie and Don with much love)

Section 5 - Passion:

Breath

For my husband who holds my heart

Y ou're there when I turn around,

When I'm stumbling and falling down,
When the weather is dull and icy,
You are my sunshine tuning out the cold,
You hold me in your arms and make all right,
In the night when it's scary and dark,
You're breathing comforts me,
And let's me know you are close,
My arm reaches out,
You snuggle in close,
I feel your breath on my neck,
And I am home.

~0~

Two Hearts

For my husband who holds my heart

I sleep better this way,

Two hearts beating as one,
Tucked close beside you,
Feeling your breath,
On my shoulder and neck,
As you inhale in and out,
Comforted to know you're there,
I feel you're every move,
As you snuggle in closer,
I smile, moving closer still,
Relaxing, knowing,
I am safe and warm,
Loved more than I can say,
I sleep,
A dreamless, deep sleep,
Awakening only to,
My skin tingling with anticipation,
As your eyes open in the morning,
I smile,
You return that smile,
You reach for me,
And we make love,
Together, always as one.
~0~

The One

For my husband who makes things easier just by being his
kind self.

A lump in my throat,

I look over at him,
Puzzled and bewildered,
Should I make the first move?
Nervous and shy,
I finally decide,
I have to make a move
What if he's the one?
I can't let go?

I smile shyly at him,
And he smiles back,
Words come unbidden,
From my tongue,
A foolish question
What's your star sign?
But he just laughs and tells me,
Asking me what's mine?
A conversation started,
An invitation to dance,
A night filled with magic,
I never want to end.

~0~

Love me and not ask why

(This is for those men who need to be told)

T here's a better way,
Without flowers and candy,
To tell me that you care,
To tell me you love me,
Or don't you dare?
Show me your emotions,
Ask me about my day,
Take me in your arms,
Out of the blue,
For I want no one but you,
I don't need jewellery or money,
I need you to let me know,
All will be okay,
That you're there,
Beside me, to offer solace,
When all I want to do is cry,
I need you to love me,
And not ask why,
But let me take you in my arms,
And share my happiness,
That you are mine,
And I am yours.
~0~

Still

(For those wanting forgiveness I wrote this)

Forget what I said earlier,
It will only make you mad,
To discover the truth,
That I'm wrong instead,
For I turn that around,
Blaming you my response,

I haven't the guts,
To admit my mistake,
For I continue bending,
Your ear with tales,
Elaborate ones, but lies,
Risking your hate,

For I love you still,
I want back the love,
I had so long ago,
The one without recriminations,
Rosy pictures, of me and you,

The view you had of me,
All sweetness and light,
Went away in all those fights,
Years of poverty and strife,
Took away my happy bubble,
I can't sustain the inner light,

I want to reach out,
And ask you to forgive,
The arguments so petty,
Just forget it all,
Please love me,

Do not withdraw,
Just take me,
In your arms,
Whisper sweet nothings,
In my ear,
And love me,
Still.

~0~

Shelter

For my husband who holds my heart

Shelter me in your arms,

Breathe life into me,
For without you,
I am empty and alone,

I need the safety of your arms,
The care you give,
Your words that keep me sane,
And feeling confidence I've never felt,

When I falter you encourage,
No longer afraid to make mistakes,
For no punishment will follow,
No laughter in my wake,
Just inspiration to try again,
And succeed like never before,
You are the sweet air, I breathe,
That keeps me going forward,
Despite all obstacles,
With you I am reborn.

~0~

Cupid' s Arrow

My heart is pierced with Cupid's arrow,
The window to seize his heart narrows,
It would appear the time is nigh,
To giggle and give my sighs,
To prance and preen my womanly charms,
But I wouldn't bet the farm,
That he will fall for me too,
For if Cupid's arrow swiftly flew,
To pierce his heart as well,
Then I would surely die,
Maybe if he had a dose,
Of my sweet potato pie,
I'd worm my way into his heart,
For Cupid would wing himself with a dart,
Through his stomach full and happy,
I better get cooking and make it snappy,
For I want to win the race,
And keep up this steady pace,
To win Cupid's heart.

~0~

Drenched in Anger

Y*ou* drench me in your anger,

As you pretend to radiate,
Your love and acceptance,
Are something to repudiate?
I am immune to *your* pretty speeches,
The candy and flowers that you bring,
I have found my sweet other,
He treats me like a partner,
Not someone on a pedestal,
To take out from a cabinet,
To admire and to brag,
I have found what I desired,
Your words hold no sway!!

~0~

Eradicated

*Y**ou* eroded my confidence,
And took my heart,
To stomp and pierce,
With pretty lies,
And sweet nothings,
Spoken in the air,
But someone stood and observed,
The lies you told,
They saw the damage you did,
They bolstered my confidence,
And with time made me see,
You were not the one for me,
He waited his time,
Captured my heart,
With his gentle thoughtful ways,
You mean nothing to me now,
But a picture in a tattered book,
Of which I never look,
Because I'm treated like an equal,
There will be no sequel,
With *you!!*

~0~

Worn and Battle Weary

For my husband who holds my heart

Y ou drag me into bliss,

Feeling I have nothing to fear,
When you mumble sweet nothings,
In my ear,
As you penetrate my defences,
You make me melt,
Into puddles of liquid,
Drawn on the spot,
You make me forget the battles,
I have fought,
You make me feel alive,
Never ever alone,
When I am with you
I hone,
On things,
That makes me whole,
Things that makes me,
A better soul,
I crave you like a firefly,
Needs the light,

For I need you,
In my sight,
Without you,
I am broken,

Hearing not all the words,
You have spoken,
To make me the strong person,
You have made me into,
Without you,
I am oh so weakened and blue,
Without you,
I am not the same person,
You see,
For I am too weary,
From battles past,
To be,
Strong alone,
So please stay with me.

~0~

Section 6 - Love

Love Is a Chain

This was written for my parent's 50th wedding anniversary. They had 53 wonderful years together cut short only by my mother's premature death. They have gone awhile know but they taught each of their children what true love is.

L ove is a long chain,
Forged link by link,
With passion and caring,
Love and sharing,
Each day brings new things to think,
New challenges and solutions,
New joys and funs,
Why it's only begun,
You as a couple have weathered the worst of life,
But you have taken the challenges and embraced
life,
And the love you share,
The ways you've showed you care,

Gave us an example,
Of the staying power of love,
Fifty years of commitment,
Your love truly heaven sent,
And this love that you've shared,
This friendship since you were nine,
Has made us all richer,
In knowing how God made you,
This special pair,
To show us what true love really is!
~0~

Valentine

I am incredibly lucky in love,
To have sent from above,
Someone who loves me, for whom I am,
And who I could become
Someone who is by my side,
Through thick and thin,
Supports me guides me,
When I need it he's there,
We are like two sides of the same coin,
One complimenting the other,
Helping each other,
Through the harshness of life,
I realize how few are given,
This gift from which I draw strength,
And I wish with all my heart,
That all could find someone,
Who loves with the intensity?
The fierce love that we have,
That supports and gives,
Life to the confidence,
That he gives me,
That being myself,

Showing myself,
To the world,
Is more than okay,
Because his acceptance,
Is all I need.
~0~

Overwhelming Love

For my husband who holds my heart and is my Valentine

I close my eyes,

Seeing you, seeing me,
For a moment,
I see myself as you see me,
I feel beautiful,
In your arms,
In your life,
Then the doubt sets in,
And I question am I worthy,
Of such a good person,
Who loves all of me?
The good the bad and the ugly,
The changeable chameleon,
That I am,
Yet you see the person,
I aspire to be,
You turn to me and say,
Never doubt you are worthy,
How did I get so lucky to have you?
And I am undone,
Overwhelmed with love for you.

~0~

To Win and Be Won

Cocooned in life,
My endless strife,
Always battles to be won,
Titles to be lost,
Whatever is to be done?
To succeed to make peace,
With life's strange master,
That pushes me one way,
Then pulls me right back,
To watch me twist and turn,
Like a ballerina on a stick,
I keep on like always,
Ever battling ever vigil,
Waiting for my chance,
To win and be won.

~0~

Smile

Smile because it free and it's catching,

Smile because it makes all things look better,
Smile because it turns a frown upside down,
Smile because it makes your wrinkles smiling
instead of frowning,
Smile because it can make someone else's world
brighter,
Smile because you are looking at your loved ones,
Smile because you're the lucky one,
Smile because it makes you happy,
Smile because it can make you beautiful,
Smile because the whole world loves a smile,
Smile because you can,
Just Smile.
~0~

Time

T ick tock tick tock,

Goes the clock,
Time racing,
Barely keep pacing,
With events,
Days seem too quickly gone,
Weekends blink and their gone,
Time speeding up,
As the years go swiftly by,
Another birthday coming,
How is possible you ask,
As you go on with your daily tasks,
But the second hand still goes round,
And you continue on with all the sound,
Not really complaining as time goes on,
Because you are here and others are not,
So you must find what the future has rought,
Achieve what you were put here to do,
Before the sand runs through.

~0~

Generosity of spirit

For my husband who holds my heart

Y̲ou have a generosity of spirit,

That's always touched my heart,
Your kindness, thoughtfulness and tender care,
Keeps me happy and going strong,
We are one,
Partners in this life,
Through adversity and strife,
I know you, as my love,
Are always there,
As I am for you,
Give and take,
We're quite a pair,
I don't know what I do,
Without you in my life,
But I know that,
I made the best decision,

To be your wife,
You bring out the best part of me,
Make me feel confident in myself,
Anything difficult is made easier,
And anything good is made possible,
With you by my side,
I am complete.
~0~

Mother Dear

T hough we live far apart,

You are always near,
Forever in my heart,
In hear your wisdom so true and bold,
In the knowledge, my children are told,
I hear your voice in my children's voice,
In every little thing, that is my choice,
You are always with me,
Even as I drink my tea,
As a mother there is no finer example than you,
Giving all your children more than their due,
Sacrificing food, money, clothing doing without,
Is it any wonder that I have to shout?
How lucky I am to have a life so blessed,
To have a mother, I must confess,
As truly wonderful as you.

~0~

Section 7 - Coming To Terms with Grief:

Mettle

The fog creeps in its snail's pace,
Makes one feel it won't embrace,
The days gathering gloom,
When it starts to zoom,
The house drips with fog filled moss,
Does it know we've suffered loss?

We struggle to lift the overwhelming pain,
But the weather suits our mood, no joy to feign,
We wish it would be lenient and carry us away,
To distant memories of joy and play,

We soldier on, memories and find delight,
In small things like flying a kite,
The whisper of a summer rain,
Takes away the pain,
The fog its seeping bone pain now gone,
The summer's sun with us all day long,

Flowers blooming, the rose's sweet scent,
Give way to smiles lent,
To brush the grief away,
To a small corner in your mind,
Seek peace and you shall find,

Relief and life proceeding,
Filling days, grief receding,
Even in life's greatest tests,
We locate our true mettle and zest,
We persevere and find comfort again,
Happiness found, true Zen,
As we move on, but never forget,
We'll meet again.

~0~

Breathe You In

Now that you are gone,

My face, feels frozen,
My heart empty,
A heavy burden,
I did not ask for,
I feel so alone,

I reach for you,
You're not there,
My heart grows heavy,
My chest feels tight,
Tears streak across,

I grieve so hard,
I think I'll die,
But the sun comes up,
The sun goes down,
And still I linger on,

Existing in place,
Though I fill numb,
I wander like a zombie,
Idling away hours,
Filling time that never ends,
Scheduling things to do,
To take my mind from you,

Days never function,
As they did.
People speak of you.
To comfort me,
Solace is not nigh,
There is only one thing,
I seek, though I cannot have,
Only in you, can I find I abide,

I stare at pictures,
Empty picture frames,
And think of you,
Morning noon and night,
Begging all the fates,
To bring you back,
But nothing changes,
To fill the void of absences,
Of lonely long nights

I inhale the fragrance.
On your pillowcase,
Unwashed for fear,
I lose the aroma,
The essence of you,

Still contained in a signal atom,
A bouquet that contains a trace,
Memory of me touching you,
Loving you, kissing you,
I breathe you in
To save the scent,

A musky smell,
That I taste on my lips,
It tangs so sweet,
Lingering on my palate,
Filling me with warmth,

It touches my tongue,
And lingers on my nostrils,
Memories flood my senses,
Of passionate nights and days,

I fall asleep the pillowcase,
Beneath my head,
And dream of you,
Alive for a few hours,
I am in your arms again,

I wish I could stay,
But morning comes,
Wide- awake,
I beg for sleep again,
Still I carry on
Alone,
Apart from you,
I hold you near,
Your pillowcase still clasped in my hand.

~0~

Ravage

Y ou have no other way out,

The die has been cast,
Your fate has been sealed,
I cannot change this disease,
That ravages you and steals from you,
Day by day away from me,
It steals first your hope,
It takes your energy,
It makes you sad,
It makes you mad,
Then takes your breath away,
Selfishly, I want to take away,
All your fears,
Your pain,
But is that for me, or you?
For I hate to see you suffer,
For I know the time will come,
That I will grieve for you,

For nothing can be done,
The cigarettes did their job,
They found another victim,
And they've moved on,
Long ago,
But the damage was done.
~0~

NB. My mom suffered first from emphysema then lung cancer from years of smoking and inhaling cigarette smoke. My dad was a chain smoker and died from lung cancer shortly after my mother died. This is what I saw with first my mother, then my father. How I wish they'd never started smoking, but you cannot change the past when they were teens smoking was considered cool.

Do Not Weep For Me

Do not weep for me,
But find the place,
Where memories lie,
Where I can live,
In sweet embrace,
Through pictures,
And through dreams,
I am with you,

When you see nature,
At its best,
I am there,
Remember,
As I watch over you,
Loving you from afar,

Smile and remember me.
For I am always with you,
That voice you hear is me,
Whispering softly guiding you,
Loving you,
Until we will meet again.
~0~

Saying Goodbye

B eauty in the soul and face,

A smile always yours to behold,

Memories will sustain you,

As the pain of loss takes hold,

Embrace the smile; lock it in your heart,

In memories you will never part.

~0~

Time Heals

T ime heals all wounds,

They say,

But what do you do?

To will the change away?

Do you simper in a corner?

Waiting for tomorrow?

Or seize the reins?

Helping with the change,

To better the future,

Move on from past,

Finding meaning for yourself,

From woes and heartache,

Pain from missing,

The person you nurtured,

At your breast,

Living their life,

While your life is stilled,

You must move on,

Finding yourself again,

And seeing hope,

For your future,

Again.

~0~

Missing You

Tired can't sleep,

Sad thoughts,

Drifting through,

My mind,

Knocking at,

My brain,

Telling me,

Like a ticking,

Time bomb,

I miss you,

I want to see you,

Time drifted away,

Since we last saw,

Each later,

But memories,

Keep us focused,

Shared experiences,

Family memories,

Deeply ingrained,

Lead me back to you,

If only in memories.

~0~

Linked

(

They were linked,

An entanglement of family bonds,

Strong and unbroken,

Untested by death's bony finger,

Until the spectre knocked at the door,

Ushered in such a quiet manner,

To steal away a member,

So loving and dear to them,

To take away a mother,

A woman getting back her life,

Her happiness after strife,

Divorce from childhood sweetheart,

A new fiancé, a man strong and kind,
Who could make her life fulfilled again,

It seemed heartless to attack her at her best,

But the illness the devourer of blood,

Had other plans, as the menace of death,

Laughed and made his plans,

A bone marrow match,

Five likely candidates to attain,

The harmonizing balance,

The spectre had his laugh,

He knew none would join,

Their blood too different,

A throwback she was,

A bone marrow match was found,

The pairing not so accurate,

Doctors considered close enough,

The blood received at baby's birth,

That made her sick, it didn't match,

Its antibodies lingered in the blood,

Cancelling out all the good,

The body attacked itself,

No measure of advantage,

In the transplanted blood,

She cried out in pain,

The body had suffered,

It withered, lingering in pain,

The spectre of death,

Took pity, on the valiant warrior,

Taking its prize,

Decimating a family,

Who took pride,

In being one.

Pulling together,

The family showed their might,

They raged against the loss,

Mourned together

Thinking often of her,

Taking care of her children,

Speaking to her,

Hoping she heard,

Their prayers of peace and love,

Each year, twice a year,

They visit her grave,

Reminding her of their love,

That she is not forgotten,

Though she may be above,

She will always be in their hearts,

Linked with them always,

In the stories they tell of her life,

And of the sibling love

She brought to their lives.

~0~

Unbreakable Bond

An unbreakable bond,

Parent to child,

Death cannot break,

Paternal or maternal hold,

Though life maybe done,

A parent watches over,

Sends love though,

We cannot see,

We feel their presence,

They have not gone,

In our darkest hours,

They love us and attend,

Grief can over take us,

And bring us low,

For we miss the counsel,

They gave us,

The love that sustains,

If we listen close,

We hear their words,

And the love remains

Forever more.

~0~

Remembering Mother

Remember her,

When time has passed,

Without tears,

For she is with you,

Always,

In the smile you see,

Upon your face,

The tilt of your head,

The voice that instructs you,

When you falter,

She is there,

For a mother never disappears,

She is at hand,

In memorics and deeds,

To guide and love you,

Forever more,

She never leaves you,

Her love is never absent,

But eternally yours.

~0~

Part of the Heavenly Choir

Mom, I hear your voice,

I turn, I look,

But it's only you,

Within a photo book,

The pages of my memories,

The fleeting snitches,

Of memories gone,

The remembrances of how lucky,

I was,

To have you for that time,

To be my mother,

How lucky we all were,

My sisters and my brothers,

How I may have taken for granted,

How as a teen I raved and ranted,

But you were always there,

To show how much you cared,

I can't believe it's been so long since,

I hugged you and looked into your face,

How I wished someone else could take your place,

You could stay here, but that was selfish,

Not what you would have wished,

You taught me things that will live on,

You taught me compassion,

Tolerance and giving of oneself,

You taught me kindness,

In and of itself,

So many people's lives you touched,

So many people miss you so much,

So Mom I hope you're celebrating with the
heavenly choir,

As they hear your harp playing and admire,

The beauty of your voice and the playing that you do,

Because if you're not with us,

It's the least than can do,

I love you,

Someday we will be together all of us and Dad too,

But until then sing sweetly and know you are always loved,

My dear mother, in heaven above.

~0~

Father

Father I hear you calling,

A whisper in the wind,

I know you still check in on me,

Peeking in from time to time,

I know you are still proud of me,

As I was always to call you Dad,

I miss your crooked smile,

And your warm blue eyes,

I miss you saying I'm your little girl,

But I know you are without pain now,

You with your best friend, Mom,

I was lucky to have the world's best Dad,

Always there for me and your other children,

You worked so hard to put food on the table,

You never thought any job to good for you,

As long as it was honest, you gave it your all,

I was oh so proud,

People who met you thought you, charming,

A loving husband,

Loyal to a fault,

To me you were just my Dad,

With whom I talked history,

Poetry too,

Listening to stories that spellbound me,

Appreciating Celtic music,

Bagpipes most of all,

You taught me so many things,

I've passed onto my children,

The one thing you taught me most,

Was generosity of spirit,

For your heart was an endless giver,

Of kindness and love,

So enjoy your time in heaven above.

Thank you, Dad!!

~0~

Lilacs

The scent of lilacs filters in my nose,

Memories come to me of old,

My grandmother shaking out her powder,

Scents of lilac or rose fill the air,

From Yardley or Avon,

The tin cleverly hidden,

In her house dress pocket proclaims,

Birthdays, the tree we would cut,

Fully bloomed lilacs,

The colours so bright,

Purple, white, and light purple,

Would adorn a mayonnaise bottle,

Proudly set in the middle of the table,

To finish a picture of happiness,

Many grandchildren offering,

Pictures lovingly drawn of spring,

Smiles exchanged,

Memories made,

Engraved in minds,

Forever more,

Lilacs their petals like silk,

The scent sweet and cloying,

As I close my eyes,

Seared memory in my brain,

Holding my grandmother,

Close to me,

Forever, more.

~0~

Christmas Loss

To some Christmas brings pain,

The ache of loss and joy to feign,

The hearts ribbons all tangled,

With the past their core mangled,

Emotions of joy remembered and lost,

Focused on the present Christmas without,

Them by their side,

For they cannot abide,

Christmas where they find no beauty,

No peace,

No joy,

Only duty,

To go on as they did like they were before,

Still they want what they had some more,

Life brings pain and loss,

Humans are resilient,

We pack the pain away,

In memories oh so tight,

Just to say

We go on and live again,

But the hurt lingers,

And sometimes dredges nigh,

With Christmas songs,

Triggering memories to come by,

We choose to pick the good and move on,

Or wallow in the memory,

That they're gone,

And lose the joy of Christmas,

All its memories,

Old and new,

We create for generations to come.

~0~

Memories

This for all those whom we have lost to soon.

P eople come into our lives,

With happiness, bliss and fun,

They bring such good things to enrich,

That they shine the sun,

We share our lives our passions,

Joys and our sorrows,

Thinking there will always be tomorrows,

But life is shorter than we know,

And disease can steal the blood's flow,

Stealing the moments,

We most enjoy,

Even take the ones that annoy,

But one thing it can't steal,

It can't take memories of moments shared,

We can tell those memories if we bear,

The fruit of a life that touched us,

Made us whole and made friends of us,

It can't seize stories we can tell,

Of good and bad and in between,

Of moments when we fell,

And were held aloft by them,

The person gone is always seen,

And live forever more.

~ 0~

Whisper

A whisper in the breeze and I hear my name,

From your lips, like it once was spoke,

Big sister advice, I hear in my head,

For memories are all I have,

Of you and what we were,

A big sister to tag along with,

Play games and dolls with,

Someone to show me fashion,

How to wear my hair,

Someone to look up to,

And know was always there,

If I needed her,

How I miss you sis,

I think of you all the time,

How it's just not fair,

That you are not here,

Too many years missed out,

Growing old and experiencing,

All the gifts that life brings,

Someday I know I'll see you again,

And we'll reminisce of the days of old,

Until then I'll look at your picture and smile,

Grateful that you were in my life.

~0~

Sisters

Sisters share our lives our joy and our sorrow,

We always think there will be a tomorrow,

To spend the time to share our days of sun and fun,

But sometimes there comes a day,

When it blocks out the sun,

Everything has stopped,

As it seems cold and gray,

Sorrow has overtaken,

What once was a ray,

But remember my friend,

Though it seems hard to believe,

Those we love don't go away,

They walk beside us every day,

Unseen, unheard, but always near,

Still loved, still missed and very dear,

Though death leaves heartache,

Seeming too much to bear,

Though we can't feel them,

Even their touch,

They are near and smiling,

At us from heaven's cloud.

~0~

Until they meet again

A door opened,

And one closed,

Hearts broken,

Eyes filled with tears,

A good man's time had come,

Too soon it seemed,

A stubborn man,

A family man,

Always at the call

Loved by his family,

One and all,

The hole he leaves,

Will not be filled,

But the memories,

Of times well-spent,

Of love and fun,

Will comfort them,

And keep them company,

Feeling the love surround them,

Until they meet again.

~0~

Section 8 - Nature

February' s Icy Blast

W inter's ice finger at our backs,

Hearts hopeful nature's greenery's rebirth is nigh,

That the groundhog didn't lie,

But February's slumbering grip,

Seizes our spirits in chill and snow,

All hope almost lost,

But still the seed blooms.

~0~

Spring Where Art Thou?

Snowflakes shaped like ornaments,

Snow is coming down,

And all I do is frown,

I want it all to go,

Not continue to blow,

Spring seems so far away,

I want to go out and play,

But snow is cold and wet,

And my mind is really set,

On the snow going far away,

I want to see the grass sway,

The grass grow green and long,

As the birds sing their song,

How I long for warm sun,

Where I can go have fun,

Walking in the woods trail,

Taking a boat out for a sail,

Go away stupid snow,

You really must go,

But I know spring is far away,

So in the snow I must play,

Or wait by the window and frown.

~0~

Snowman

Snowman here I come,

I'm going to make some,

But the snow isn't right,

And with it I fight,

If only the snow was soft,

Then I might be able to aloft,

On a toboggan down the hill,

Riding, gliding take my fill,

Of winters total fun,

Even enjoying the sun,

But the snow is hard and wet,

And all I really seem to get,

Is miserable and cold,

As into my bed I fold,

To get warm and dry,

Oh please time fly,

To spring,

Bring it to me,

Now.

~0~

Little Robin Red Breast

Little robin red breast,

Bobbing your head up and down,

Looking in the cold wet ground,

Some small morsel,

You've found,

In the warm spring sun,

The snow recedes leaving,

Puddles in its wake,

You dip your feathers,

In the gleaming wet chilly pool,

Shiver and shaking,

You dig once again,

At the foot,

Of the old withered tree,

Hoping for berries,

Forgotten, but wintering there,

Little red breasted robin,

Heralding the spring,

Opening your mouth,

You sweetly sing.

~0~

Springtime

Grasses blowing in the breeze,

Soft wind blowing stalks to and fro,

Trees green and towering full and tall,

Beauty seen across the sight line,

Brook babbling clear and cold,

Fisherman casting their lines,

People picnicking happy and warm,

Frisbees being thrown toss back and forth,

Children swinging, laughing running about,

Fun frolicking in the sun like time has just begun,

Sun kissed skin glowing with health,

People wake up from their slumbering winter,

To come alive it's a warm spring day,

And winter cares are sent away.

~0~

Spring

Irises softly blowing,

Seeds softly sowing,

In the rain,

Hitting my window pane,

Grass, green and lush,

It's almost too much,

As the wind blows,

And water flows,

In rivets along the ground,

As the ants move up in a mound,

A small frog hops about,

Keeping dry,

Drenched wet clothes underneath my umbrella,

Wishing that I was walking with my fella,

Wishing for a hot drink,

Instead of feeling like I'm in a sink,

Squishy socks, sloshing shoes,

I'm all wet, what have I to lose?

As I scurry, hurry, to and fro,

Water running down my big toe,

The ducks and geese swimming in the park,

Spread their wings in the rainy dark,

As water pools about the slide,

Causing a huge divide,

Between the swings and climbing vine,

The birds do sit and dine,

On sapling seeds and forgotten scraps,

As they bathe and their wings do flaps,

Spring has sprung its beauty to behold,

New hints of birth still untold,

As the birds make nests out of string,

Yes, spring is having its fling,

As the April showers,

Bring their May flowers,

It's spring unfurled in all its glorious beauty,

As Mother Nature, fulfills her awesome duty,

Colour, everywhere I look.

~0~

Mountain Fed Spring

I want to go to the mountain fed spring,

Lie upon the fresh grass,

As the brook water laps,

As the sun beats down,

A fresh breeze blows,

Through my hair,

I want to stare up at the sky,

Watch the clouds roll by,

Then look over at the mountain,

In the distance and breath in the fresh air,

As spring has sprung,

My youth is remembered.

~0~

Bitter

Bitter is the perfume,

Glorious in its fragrance,

The budding blooms of spring,

As a stumble,

Tissue to my nose,

Sneezing repeatedly

Still I find my lips,

Widening,

I smile,

At the flourishes of spring.

~0~

Goslings

The little birds' heads pop up,

In the thick grass by the roadside,

The mother goose herds them to sup,

From bugs on the other side,

The cars stop and stare as the goslings,

Waddle across, mama herding her babies,

Across to the road,

Where the food does abide,

Their tuffs of yellow,

So pretty make you mellow,

As you watch them and smile,

As the smallest one sits on a pile,

Of wildflowers bright blue,

Nature's best it's true,

The cars pass on the scene goes on,

The food is exhausted there's still a bond,

As Mama birds and babies,

Move on and on.

~0~

Rebirth

Thundering skies, light flashes,

Twisting, turning sideways,

Winding, downward it slides.

Hitting the ground with force,

As the ground trembles in its wake,

Animals frightened scurrying to and fro,

Mother Nature flings barns trees, buildings,

Like they were discarded playthings,

As it passes people survey the loss,

Coming sorrowfully together,

To begin and help a new,

As rebirth begins,

Found in fellowship,

And ingenuity,

By men and women,

Life goes on

~0~

Summer's Kiss

Summer's kiss,

Sometimes it's bliss,

Sun shining,

Birds singing,

Heat rising and beating down,

Makeup running, like on a clown,

Children playing in the hose,

Laughing and waiting in a pose,

To feel the cool water rush,

And summer's heat flush,

Away as childhood memories made,

As mother does swiftly bade,

Fill up the pool and waste water not,

As she brings out Popsicles sought,

The day drags on the children drag out bikes,

The little ones beg for their trikes,

They tear up and down sidewalks,

As the mothers and fathers continue talks,

In patios and front verandas swings,

As some sneak in for air conditioning,

As the heat's fury is dealt,

Summer's kiss is felt.

~0~

Blue Skies

Blue skies towering above,

Feeling my heart with love,

For nature's beauty that surrounds,

For nature's beauty that astounds

To look up and see clouds flowing by,

Marshmallow and white oh so high,

I feel myself floating in my imagination,

Soaring through the sky over nations,

Free to fly,

Flying high,

Seeing the beauty of it all,

Before I fall,

Painting it with my words,

To last forever and a day.

~0~

Nature Thwarted

Branches fallen wind rising,

Car veering on the road,

Rain pelting down,

A dark cloud on the horizon,

Touching the ground,

Waterspouts out on the lake,

Wind still rising,

Hydro towers tumbling,

Like tiny little blocks,

Nature's power behold,

As it unfolds,

Darkness at the venue,

Music unheard,

People crowded in the dark,

Waiting to surprise,

Birthday boy arrives,

Too much fanfare,

Is truly surprised,

In the dark,

People having fun,

Talking here and there,

Enjoying company,

Who needs the light anyway?

~0~

Resilience

Massive ruin lies in wait,

As clouds form,

Thunder rumbles,

Flashes lightning so bright,

Clouds joining together,

Forming a funnel so big,

That they buckle under the strain,

Wind bustles through,

Flattening trees, plants,

Buildings in its path,

Minutes pass,

The wind dissipates,

The sun comes out,

People crying, praying,

Laughing with joy,

At finding loved ones,

Had survived,

Rebuilding in the same place,

Hopeful that it won't happen again,

But still the wind blows,

Only sirens warning,

The call to arms.

~0~

Autumn

W aning hot breath of summer,

Giving birth to leaves,

Of green, gold, orange,

Red, and brown, fall leaves,

Trees sway, leaves fall,

Cold crisp days begin,

The cool air strokes

Your lungs,

It feels good,

To be alive,

Squirrels gathering their nests,

Geese getting their fill,

Of grasses sweet and clean,

Birds ready to fly,

To pastures warm and dry,

For winter will come,

The ground will gather frost,

The snow will fall,

Covering the then hard ground,

Until then we enjoy,

The colours and sensations of fall,

Alive in the moment,

Smiling at it all.

~0~

Winter' s Embrace

C olour flows in the wind,

I gaze in wonder outside,

The colours stimulate a smile so wide,

I see the rest of the leaves,

Getting ready to fall,

Sunflowers so beautiful and tall,

The other flowers brown and weary,

Making me slightly teary,

As the roses fade away,

One last gasp before winters freeze,

No more buttercups to make me sneeze,

The grass is green, but soon will brown,

As frost covers the scorched, tired earth,

I get ready to enjoy home and hearth,

And snuggle down in warmed domicile,

To watch the weather outside from window sill,

And get ready to play in winter's wonderland.

~0~

Icy Finger of Snow

Snow drifting weaving its icy finger,

Cold wet and dissolving at the touch,

It lingers for a moment in the sky,

Then free falling to the ground,

Snowflakes falling a long way down,

The swirly way it falls,

Huge flakes spun like sugar,

Whirling, winding, twisting, down

As you imagine it,

Dancing on your tongue,

So cold and wet,

Outside is all white,

Such a pretty sight,

When you're sitting safe and warm,

A blanket across your lap,

The snow continues falling,

It piles up so high,

You think about the shovelling,

You wonder why,

You ever thought it pretty,

Yet the beauty captures,

Your inner child,

Who quivers with glee,

As the trees laden with snow,

Their branches dip and shake,

The snow continues to fall,

People stop and look,

The snows topping them in their wake,

The cars spurt and sputter,

The roads grow thick impassable,

All you can see is white,

As car stall and people,

Make their way to shelter,

A picture post card at your feet,

A Christmas card in your eyes,

A glow in Christmas lights,

The snow softly falls.

~0~

Blood Moon

B lood moon,

Scary sight,

Like a red planet,

In the night,

Total lunar eclipse moon,

Darkened by the shadow,

Of the Earth,

First in a tetrad,

In two thousand fourteen,

Doom theories abound that,

Historical events surround,

The rising of the lunar eclipse,

Biblical theory of apocalypse,

Also known as Hunter's moon,

Light so red and bright,

All the animals,

Scurry out of sight,

Fear not,

Troubled men,

Of this awesome sight,

Of fire and light,

It's merely a phenomenon,

Of sunrises and sunsets,

Glinting off the earth,

Light and shadow's red return,

Simply a colored moon,

Shining above.

~0~

Life in the Dark

People say life in the dark,

Is boring and lonely,

And sometimes it is,

But if you use your ears,

You can hear,

The sounds of nature,

The whisper of the breeze,

Flowing through the branches,

Twigs hitting the eaves,

Banging garbage cans,

Raccoons forage for their meal,

People in their backyards,

Trying to keep their voices low,

But not succeeding,

Talking and laughing,

The smell of a backyard fire,

Roasting marshmallows,

Flowing through the wind,

A nip of autumn in the air,

The noises die down,

The reverberating sound,

Of a slamming door,

Night sounds are beautiful,

As the quiet hour approaches,

Only the sound of crickets,

And tree frogs are heard,

The velvet black sky,

Twinkles with stars,

Planets masquerade,

Lighting the atmosphere,

Night is neither boring, nor lonely

With such, beauty to behold.
~0~

Garden Pests

B lue skies,

Fresh dirt,

Flowers' roots,

Reaching for water,

Birds flying,

In for the kill,

Wiggling worms,

Pulled up,

From the ground,

Bunnies exiting burrows,

Hopping across lawns,

To score the carrots,

In the woman's garden,

Woman loudly whining,

No carrots for her this year,

Flowers would have to do.

~0~

Summer

The glow of the sun,

Almost a metallic gold,

Shimmers emitting radiance,

That beckons ones' eyes,

Despite the relentless squinting,

To the bright light,

The surface that we,

Once thought polished,

Pitted and crated,

Beautiful making,

All creatures feel alive,

Living things growing,

Reaching high,

Corn stalks on the rise,

Summer is here,

As we soak up the sun,

Kissed and loved by its light,

We feel more alive,

Hoping we won't get burnt,

But enjoying it anyway.

~0~

Morning Surprise

Every morning's dash,

Preferring to linger,

Over coffee and sunrise,

Still they dart,

To the car,

Off to work,

The front door opens,

A bird following impulse,

Lays an egg,

Then takes to sky,

Commuter looks over,

In the garden,

A present hauntingly beautiful,

A morning surprise,

An egg found.

~0~

Roses

Roses sweet their cloying perfume,

Essence of passion and love,

Thorns hidden within.

~0~

Managing the Cold

Barren landscape,

Coming soon,

Scenes of white,

Intense bitter cold,

Worry of heating bills,

So astronomically high,

Blankets for the living room,

Thermostat turned to low,

Blankets on the bed,

On our laps watching television,

We manage the cold

~0~

Poor Postie

Snow feathery and light,

Falling down,

Furiously, continuously,

Accelerating as it blows around,

Mounting up upon the ground,

Soon despite the pain,

I'll be shoveling to find the driveway,

The walkway must be found,

Or the poor postie,

Will not come to my door,

Through drifts so high,

Why couldn't the snow be passive?

Instead it's gone all rogue,

Storming continuously, week after week,

Even the groundhog has gone to ground,

Hiding until the sun will shine,

And warmth will come,

In the promise of spring,

It's the groundhog, Willie;

Or some other herald, we blame,

But maybe they had it right,

And we should all do the same,

Hiding in our homes,

Until spring comes again,

~0~

Snow Shovelling

Snow shovelling,

The bane of my life,
The digging, oh the strife,
It looks so pretty and oh so bright,
The glittering flowing,
Way it falls,
Within my sight,
But then reality sets in,
I realize how much digging,
I have to do,
To find the driveway,
And the walkway,
It's under there somewhere,
I know I'll find it,
I know I will.

~0~

Snow

G liding, flowing swiftly down,

Floating softly to the ground,

No single flake alike,

The joy on a face of a tyke,

As they catch some on their tongues,

And cold air fills their lungs,

As they happily cry,

Winter has come.

~0~

Mother Nature

Mother Nature has pulled off quite the joke,

Making the humans think it is spring,

With winter's wallop on the way,

A mix of rain and ice, with snow to stay,

For those who thought spring to remain,

A huge laugh at our expense,

Mother Nature is angry and rightfully so,

We've ravished her earth savagely,

And put her in a rage,

She's not charming anymore,

But simply on the prowl,

To get even with us,

For our evil deeds,

Hopefully we can charm,

And get in a better mood,

So we can survive,

Her anger before it,

Implodes and takes us,

To weather we've never seen,

And places we don't want to go.

~0~

Winter

The once blue sky,

Is gray and dismal,

The clouds low,

Heavy with snow,

Sunshine is not to perceived,

Even in the lull,

Of snow, not falling,

But ready to go,

The trees once luscious,

And dark green,

Now have no leaves,

To be seen,

Just bare branches,

No snow can break,

The ice thickening,

On the lake,

Calls its siren,

To the hearty few,

As fishing and playing,

Hockey ensues,

No waffling,

Accepting winter is here,

Let's get outside and enjoy it,

No need to fear,

The cold as we bundle up,

Bravely claim the key,

Hello and welcome winter,

For we're Canadians you see.

~0~

Environment

D ecrepit bones older than their age,

Credible evidence the environment,

Has condemned the owner to its pain,

Pensively the holder wonders what causes all,

Products grown with chemicals,

To keep the bugs and disease away,

Have cross-pollinated,

The offending foods,

Making some allergic,

To its nourishment,

Should the possessor eat,

Of processed foods,

The body it offends,

With swift justice,

Headaches will ensue,

Swelling of face and throat,

Just to name a few,

What's a person to do?

To escape this circle,

Of everlasting blame?

Why grow their own crops,

Make their bread by hand,

Make all their foods their selves,

Except their energy is low,

They haven't strength to save themselves,

So soon off this world to soon they'll go,

The environment does offend.

~0~

Thunderstorms

T hunder and fury,

Rain cascades down,

Filling up the caked earth,

With nature's life blood,

Lightning striking to give birth,

To nutrients that enrich the soil,

Making the crops grow,

To start the cycle of life again.

~0~

Autumn

Autumn leaves drifting round,

Spinning, spiralling, falling down,
Colours erupting, a beautiful sight,
Orange, green, red sheer delight,
Children playing in leaves piled high,
Screams of glee,
The leaves continue to fall,
The rake stand idle,
The bags not full,
The children complain,
As father reaches out,
Rake in hand,
Scooping leaves
Paper bags now full,
The beautiful leaves gone,
The children pray and wait,
For more leaves to fall,
And playing in the leaves,
To begin again.

~0~

Perspective

T he wind blows,

The trees shake,

Their leaves flowing down,

The pine tree shakes its needles loose,

Like fine green moss it covers the grass,

The sky is dark and ominous as the rain,

Pelts down sideways as it falls on the plain,

Umbrellas turning inside out, tempers fraying,

While a small child laughs in glee,
Her raincoat buttoned high

Her tiny feet encased in boots

That splash and putter in the water

To her happy sweet little cries

~0~

Pity the Weatherman

T hey say it's depraved,

To predict a powerful storm,

That doesn't come,

Only some odd flakes,

But weather isn't an exact science,

It can jump and skip,

Localities focus on one,

For the cold winds still blow,

And silly people,

Still don't listen and die,

The snow mounts up,

The sea-walls break,

Ice and water fill sea towns,

People resilient and resourceful,

Some shovel the snow,

With large contraptions,

Some hunker down and stay warm,

Others take up winter sports,

For the cold winds,

Still blow, whistling down hills,

The snow still falls,

In huge bitter icy flakes,

But the snow will end,

And life goes on,

Pity the poor weatherman,

So misunderstood,

Yet again.
~0~

Section 9 - Philosophy and other Thoughts

Onward to Mackie's

Mackie's is a wonderful beach restaurant in Port Stanley Ontario. It's been at the beach forever it seems and will celebrate its 107th birthday this year. If you go there be sure to try the fries, the orangeade and of course the secret Mackie's sauce.

As I amble down the road,

My car pointed to the beach,

Unfurled are,

Sunny skies,

Green fields,

As far as the eye,

Can see,

The sun beating down,

Warming the skin,

Wonderful is how,

I feel,

Flowers blooming,

Trees sprouting,

Farmer's fields becoming alive,

As sprouts come up to kiss the sun,

Birds their wings unfurled,

As the summer world,

Wakes up to new life,

And new love and new sights,

Of wonder to see,

To the earth's edge,

Where sky meets shimmering water,

Pleasure boats sail by,

Sand is flung to and fro,

Frolicking, laughing children,

Enjoy surf and sun,

Wet bathing suit clad people,

Beachgoers,

Saunter gleefully by,

Enjoying the cool waters,

Even as they shiver and wonder why,

They took the dip that made them cold,

They shake out their towels,

And warm themselves,

As they wander down the beach to Mackie's,

And enjoy the fries and Orangeade,

To celebrate Mackie's years,

And wish them many, many, more,

So they can have the time,

To share with grandchildren, and friends,

Forever more,

~0~

The Great Unknown

T ime seems infinite,

And yet it's never enough,

To spend with and weather,

Life's ups and downs,

Time is assigned in,

Some unknown quantity,

That gives small amounts to some,

And larger amounts to others,

And yet in the end,

The clock stops ticking,

The body fails,

We all go into that goodnight,

The great unknown,

That we all transverse alone.

~0~

Reflection in the Mind's Eye

A reflection in the mirror,

I don't recognize,

It's not the me,

I see,

I see youth without wrinkles,

Smiles and no frowns,

I see a woman dancing,

Happy as a clown,

I see a whirlwind dervish,

Flitting from place to place,

Not this slow moving woman,

With life's map upon her face,

I discard the mirror's reflection,

And in my mind's I take,

The person young, thin and pretty,

A person who used to be witty,

At least in her mind,

That's the me,

I find,

Living within,

And share with the world.

~0~

Avenging Angel

*This is what I hope happens when conman seek to
trick others from the angel's point of view.*

I follow the sorrow,

The scripture-slinging man,

Who slithers from town to town,

The con man who slithers in,

Taking money from the pockets,

Of the poor and anxious,

To get the cures which elude them,

Carefully planning out every detail,

In advance, of how this will,

Achieve his ends,

Offers friendship and fellowship,

To the lonely and desperate,

The shut-ins and the ill,

The neglected seniors,

The tents are crammed,

Ripe bodies eager for redemption,

The revivals in full force,

The music fills the rafters,

The preacher captures his audience,

First with anecdotes of funny stories,

He humanizes himself,

As he lists the sins,

Of the audience,

He mimics the emotions,

They want to hear,

For he feels them not,

He pounds the pulpit,

For he is volatile,

Prone to emotional outbursts,

He promises fire and brimstone,

To the false prophets,

The untrue non-following few,

He then promises salvation,

To the faithful,

Who give freely,

Generously to his coffers,

For he claims,

Only the loyal,

The devoted disciples,

Of God's word shall,

Achieve the kingdom of heaven,

He has distorted,

The word of God,

For his own profit,

Viewing the innocent victims,

As inhuman objects,

To be tormented and violated,

For his amusement and his pocket,

How he laughs in private,

When he convinces them,

He has cured their woes,

Or their body's pain,

And sickness,

Only to ask them,

For their life's savings in return,

Putting those thirty pieces of silver,

Golden chalices passed around,

For he is a greedy dog,

Who can never have enough,

Who preys on shepherds,

That cannot understand,

The evil that he is,

He looks to his own way,

Every one for gain,

From every quarter,

The simple truth?

He is a psychopath,

Sent by the devil,

And I the avenging angel,

Sent to clean up his messes,

The destruction he leaves,

In his wake,

The heartache and the sorrow,

Sown and reaped,

Are mine to take,

Relieving,

The gentle trusting souls,

Of the burden,

I lift their spirits,

And their feet,

Caring them,

To bring light,

Into their lives,

And steer them,

To their local,

Communities' churches,

Where hope and faith,

Charity are born,

Renewed in their faith,

For the greatest of these is love,

For love that is shared,

With kindness, friendship,

And fellowship,

In these,

True humanity is born.

~0~

Love me, still

Why are you aloof?

Is it just temporary?

A fix so you can't see me?

As you once did?

Did I hurt you so bad?

I wish I could make you whole,

But then you'd love me again,

And that wouldn't do,

I think I much prefer this new you,

Yet some selfish part of me,

Wishes you'd love me still.

~0~

Spark

S park,

Amicable

Not frivolous,

Caring,

The villains think these,

People,

Hurt and broken,

The kind ones,

Find,

Motives,

Questioned,

By unrefined,

Careless,

People,

Who think,

In their minds,

Kindness,

Is for trampling,

In their minds,

Using these,

Vapid pathetic,

People,

At their command,

And their ends,

A right,

Twisting goodness,

And goodwill,

Until the prey,

Feel used up,

And empty,

Their kind natures,

Buried,

But villains have,

Not won,

A tiny spark,

Of kindness remains,

Germinating,

To rise again,

And bloom,

Forever more,

Generation,

After generation,

The gene of kindness,

Wills out,

In the end.

~0~

Calculating

You can be calculating,

I can be envious,

Of the easy way,

You capture people's hearts,

They cannot see your scheming,

The way you shun the messy details,

Of life, leaving strings of hearts,

For others to pick up and fix,

You go through life,

A bull in a china shop,

Well-liked well-loved

And it's never enough

For within you is a well

Never filled, always empty

Your reach always grasping

Taking, taking, taking,

And yet some part of me,

Feels sorry for you,

You are surrounded by people,

Yet always alone,

What will you have?

When life is gone?

A life full of empty promises,

Forgotten when all is done.

~0~

Heart's Desire

A tempting morsel,

She dekes and ducks,

As she willows and weaves,

Her wiles,

Her plan,

Breathtaking beautiful,

In its simplicity,

She achieves

Her heart's desire,

~0~

Respect

I can hear your raspy voice,

Demanding respect,

You demand submission,

For you mistake my meekness,

For subservience and duty,

Only to you,

A thing you own,

Not love,

But I do not like to be obedient,

It's a somber way,

Of taking control,

Of my thoughts and desires,

For respect is earned,

If you want to be esteemed,

Show me you can be,

A partner not a King.

~0~

Connected

I am invisible,

You cannot see,

What I see,

You think you understand,

But you don't,

For I feel detached,

Like I am not here,

Sometimes,

I am alone,

Shivering in the coldness,

Of isolation,

Cast into the house,

No travels for me,

For it is winter,

Or summer,

Holding me back,

The weather that hurts and harms,

You can't see that,

I just wilt,

And wither on the vine,

My desire to reach out,

And seek friendship,

Human contact,

A computer with internet,

The only other people,

To whom I speak,

Strangers, yet considered friends,

I seek enlightenment,

Knowledge and different cultures,

To fill my time,

Fill my need,

For my gregarious nature,

Craves to speak with others,

Something inside my home,

I am denied,

From time to time,

So I write humans to interact with,

Books for others to read,

Poetry to share my feelings,

My contact with others connected,

If only through words my emotions flow,

Finding the heart and minds of humankind.

~0~

You Don't Own Me!!

I sought the warmth,

Of your supple body,

Your arms that kept me safe,

But it's was all an illusion,

For you were arrogant,

And so full of charm,

And even as I bond with you,

Crudely, craftily, you separate me,

From friends and my family,

I cannot see anyone but you,

For you've mistaken love,

For title and ownership,

Your ring on my finger,

Burns a brand,

I sought to leave you,

And you made your move,

You beat me and dragged me back,

Convinced me that I was wrong,

Until you hit me yet again,

And I left scarred and scared,

But sure I don't,

Want you anymore,

You stalked me,

And I'm frightened,

You seemed everywhere,

You wanted to take me prisoner,

For you broke into my apartment,

But my pistol shot you dead,

Nightmares left in your wake,

You haunted me in my waking dreams,

No more romance for me,

No trust left in relationships,

I went on in shadowed existence,

Like you owned me still,

Voices raised in anger,

Don't frighten me anymore,

For I've taken back my life,

Taken back my power,

I learned to trust again,

I've found someone,

To trust who treated me,

Like an equal,

Who loves me, for me,

Warts and all,

He allows me to be me,

No stalking involved.

~0~

Nurturer

Is it risky behaviour?

Does it put one in jeopardy?

To open your heart and mind,

To others opinions,

Contrary to your own,

Their needs and wants,

Coming before your own,

To be a nurturer,

Can be cathartic,

Or can lead you,

Down a path,

Of endless neediness,

With your own needs forgotten,

Where do you draw the line?

Some people who don't understand ask,

Some can never pull back,

For it's in their nature,

To nurture and reach out,

I'd rather nurture then,

Turn my head and be blind,

But I've had to learn,

To be a little selfish,

Pull back sometimes too,

To protect myself,

So I'm not forgotten

Among those others'

Needs and wants

But its near impossible to.

~0~

Parasites

We are parasites,

Blights upon the world,

Sucking up resources,

Faster than they can replace,

We're tumbling towards destruction,

An explosive sight we'll be ours,

When all to sustain us are gone,

Even that which is adequate,

Cannot save our plight,

Like the dodo bird tumbling,

Towards a precipice,

For our existence will be gone,

In the blink of an eye,

All departed,

Like we never were,

So some think to enjoy,

The moment until it's gone,

But maybe we should try,

To save us from ourselves,

Save the world,

From our perilous predicament,

Let's make it our fight,

Before it's too late.

~0~

Cloak of Invisibility

Invisibility my cloak as I go through life,

Sometimes it seems though I reach out,

No one answers, no one is aware,

The world turns the day goes on,

But still I remain hidden,

Through no fault of my own,

I move through a sea of people,

No movement of their eyes,

No acknowledgement I'm there,

Just continued conversation,

To each other, favors to them returned,

But I am alone cloaked in obscurity,

Once in a while the curtain lifts,

I am remembered, a fleeting thought,

But I am more like the observer,

Seeing and not being seen,

In the end their lives take over,

I am the forgotten one.

Someday I will be remembered,

When time flows by,

And time has run out,

The curtain of invisibility ended,

Too late to make a difference,

For I will be gone.

~0~

Protest?

I am drenched in tears,

As I watch the scene unfold,

The other London burning,

A terrible sight to behold,

Questions enter my mind,

How could they burn and pillage?

My families' old time village?

Why does this happen?

When a peaceful protest held,

Why are some hooligans compelled?

What doesn't someone illuminate?

Their sense of rationality,

Or are they immune?

As they luminate?

For it is clear they radiate hate,

They don't care about their fate,

Are they immune to the sorrow?

They spread not caring for tomorrow?

My heart is drenched with tears,

And I am filled with fears,

As I watch such strife and turmoil,

As I worry about the good people of London.

~0~

Void

S tanding in a void looking out,

Wondering how to venture away,

Out of the cyclone pulling me down,

Hiding me, making me imperceptible,

See through, discernible to only a few,

Wanting to be seen, talked, to noticed,

Feeling like shouting, screaming, yelling,

Instead puzzling, swallowing and frowning,

Acceptance, unseen, somehow unworthy,

Forgotten, watching in invisibility.

~0~

The Watcher

I am the watcher,

Seen, but unseen,

Drifting through life,

Two places at once,

In the moment,

Feeling it all,

Sometimes safely removed,

Oddly detached,

Recording it all,

Yet times in the fracas,

Feeling it all,

For I feel deeply,

Every barb, every arrow,

Of scorn and derision,

Every accidental spoken blow,

Every intentional barb,

Burns through me,

Like a thousand fires,

I feel joy to excess,

Like I've climbed a mountain high,

A candle burning bright,

At both ends,

My emotions overtake me,

I must pull myself back,

Become the watcher,

In the corner,

Dullard and steadfast.

~0~

Section 10 - War and Remembrance

Remembrance Day

Y oung men eager to start an adventure,

As they face their greatest fear,

To leave kith and kin without censure,

To fight the greatest foe,

Off to the front, the war they go,

The young and the old leave their families,

Going to foreign lands, they take their leaves,

Women volunteered and were put behind the scenes,

To bandage the weary troops and keep the papers
forwarded,

With the orders down the line, and to keep the
troops boarded,

They stepped up those valiant women with none
rewarded,

The men the battle waged, battling falling in foreign
land,

Some in lonely countryside, some in Dieppe's
watery sand,

Their youth, the strength given for their country,

So we can have freedom to live and breathe and see,

A world of peace and feel that we are free,

To speak our minds and raise our families,

They gave their lives their body and mind,

To save our country, to give us time to find,

Our place in the world without oppression,

To save us from someone else's obsession,

Who wanted to control the world and control
thought,

So our troops volunteered and so valiantly fought,

Giving to us their country the peace we sought,

We thank them for their sacrifice,

Though it barely does suffice,

We thank them for the time they gave,

We thank them for the lives they save,

We thank them truly, for the battles fought,

The battles won, for the peace we sought,

We remember those who made the ultimate
sacrifice,

Though our thanks barely suffice,

And those that come home broken,

We give to all of you this token,

Of our love and remembrance

For every day that is hence,

We will remember and celebrate your life,

We remember how you had such strife,

To give us freedom and peace,

To let the hostilities cease,

Thank-you is all I can say,

Thank-you to each and every one of you

Each and every day

~0~

D-Day Remembered
~Juno Beach

Juno beach proud men,

Brave strong fearless,

Bonded for life,

No grumbling,

Though it wasn't painless,

Memories haunting them, still.

Juno Beach, a watery grave,

Boats destroyed, ninety landing craft in all,

Men loaded down with equipment,

Their bodies some sank,

Memories haunting them, still.

Bodies floating on water,

As surviving troops advanced,

Stretched across the fifty mile shore,

Bodies strewn across the beach,

Looking on in horror,

Memories haunting them, still.

As they thought,

Poor men, poor devils,

And guiltily thought

Thank God, it's not me,

Memories haunting them, still.

Parachutists falling and failing,

As the surf broke the coast,

Many missing targets,

And drowning in fields,

Memories haunting them, still

Gliders aborting others,

Shot on the way down,

Crawling out of wreckage,

To soldier on, doing duty,

Memories haunting them, still.

Taken captive by enemy,

Prisoners in this stage,

In this passage of time,

No balm to the recollections,

Memories haunting them, still.

Those that survived,

Remember those comrades,

They lost that day,

As time lingers on,

Memories haunting them, still.

Those who gave their all,

For King and country,

We remember but also,

Those that suffered,

Memories haunting them, still.

We thank them for,

Making our country,

Whole and safe,

From tyranny and strife,

Even as memories haunting them, still.

We thank them for,

Fighting the good fight,

For making Canada, remarkable,

As citizens who care.

We thank them, still.

~0~

True Patriot Love

For Corporal *Nathan Cirillo* and Warrant Officer *Patrice Vincent* who gave
their life to protect their country, Canada from terrorists. We shall never
forget!!

T rue patriot love,

Mere words to some,

But not to you,

You sacrificed,

With your life,

To protect your country,

Can we ask a greater love?

Of nation?

The men who took your lives,

Should be forgotten,

We shall triumph over their tyranny,

Their radicalization of youth,

To harm those who speak,

For our freedoms,

Your deaths a painful reminder,

That there are those who,

Seek to harm the good,

The brave, the protectors,

Your valour and sacrifice,

For your country,

Shall never be forgotten,

But remembered for all time,

Your country owes you a debt,

That cannot be repaid,

Tears fall from our eyes,

Though your earthly disposition passes,

Our love for you will remain,

Passed on for generations,

The remembrance of the lives,

Taken too soon,

Maybe by then peace will refrain,

Through all the world too.

~0~

We Remember

T hey dreamed of peace,

They dreamed of life,

Like yours and mine,

Freedoms to speak,

Freely and speak,

Loudly, if they wished,

A short time ago,

They worked hard,

Playing hard,

Spent time with family,

Fighting hard and long,

To achieve those freedoms,

Fighting and killing others,

Hurting their very souls,

Fighting to save their countries,

From tyranny and evil intent,

They gave up their home lives,

Their families and soil,

To fight for kin and country,

To save the world,

They gave much,

Now we revere them,

Remember them ,

Immortalize them,

We shall not forget,

Their sacrifice,

From sun up,

To sundown,

Each day we remember,

Their forfeit,
And honour their lives,

Remembering,
Always.
~0~

H - Bomb

I am not denigrating the contributions the soldiers made, I honour those, but I will never agree with the dropping of this bomb on Japan and the innocent lives it harmed. This poem describes what happened to those people in Hiroshima and Nagasaki and how we should never let it happen again.

The air raids sounded,

They heard the planes,

Three single planes,

Flying, soaring above,

What damage could they do?

That hadn't been done?

The leaflets rained upon them,

Days ago,

Warning of danger from a blast,

But how could one liberated bomb,

Do much damage?

They'd survive still,

The planes got closer,

They heard the roar,

The sound of propellers,

Filling their ears,

Their eyes searched for gunfire,

Their sight obscured by sun,

The bomb slowly dropped,

With a flash, so bright,

Like fireworks in their sight,

Of a thousand suns,

A cloud of dust and dirt,

Erupted to the sky,

A terrible deafening sound,

Heard, reverberating to,

A muddy, mushrooming cloud,

Eighty thousand people,

Incinerated on the spot,

People fleeing,

With burning flesh, peeled back,

Like an onion in a pot,

Living pieces of charcoal,

Walking, shocked, mindless until collapse,

Hospitals obliviated, in seconds gone,

Brave people advanced forth,

Helping those they could,

No equipment, no help,

No peace, only pain,

From a vicious bomb,

No place to treat the dead and dying,

No knowledge of the cure,

For radiation poisoning,

Ate at the bodies,

Of those who survived,

The first shockwave,

Died violently days later,

Vomiting their insides,

Some lucky souls,

Saved by walls,

Not so lucky,

It seemed,

For radiation remained,

Trapped in thyroids,

Escaping a year,

Or years later,

To take its prize,

What prize humanity for the dropping of this bomb?

What wickedness lurks in men's hearts?

That such evil can be done?

Never again should be the cry,

Never again such malevolence,

Should be used,

Remember those August days,

When innocent people paid,

For others actions,

Of people with might,

Great sin was done,

To guiltless children, young and old,

Many innocent people paid,

Their futures stolen,

And the innocence of men.

~0~

A Hundred Years

A hundred years or more,

Over a hundred years passed,

Judgement has been made,

Of what started the war,

What gains were made?

While the reasons still linger.

For others cry to war,

Pandora's Box opened,

Some war still goes on,

The war would be over by Christmas,

Was the hue and cry,

As young men heeded the call,

To arms for King and country,

But the battle raged on,

Four years and more,

Hardship and strife,

Changed family life,

Food rations and sacrifices,

The people endeavoured to go on,

Socks knitted, scarfs too,

Everything for the troops abroad,

Fourteen million lives lost,

Twenty eight countries mourned,

The loss of fathers and sons,

Husbands gone, women must go on,

As children grew up without fathers,

Life went on, but still behind the scenes,

The battle raged on,

People dissatisfaction, hurts and wounds,

Still lingered on,

Long memories, wounds never forgotten,

Territories demanded, the battle wages on,

Innocent lives taken, shortened by war,

The battles rage on,

Can we not have peace?

Must we always wage war?

The war was over a hundred years ago,

Still the battles rage on!

I am not denigrating the contributions the soldiers made, I honour those. In all, about 620,000 Canadians enlisted during the war and about 419,000 went overseas. About 60,000 would never come home. We became a country proud and strong and a national identity; but still there is war in the Ukraine, Libya, and the Gaza strip and of course in Afghanistan, Syria and other countries. People need to not worry about territory and religious differences so much and worry more about people and how many lives are being lost.

~0~

Carnage of War

Memory is a tricky thing,

Some things you believe,

Are too hard to remember,

The memories hard to bear,

Like the carnage of war,

As the cannons fire,

The smell of sulphur in the air,

The sound of muskets cutting flesh,

And the battlefield with bodies strewn,

Good men and women fought,

And died for love of country,

They deserve remembrance,

They deserve more than a day,

To be revered and accolated,

To have their resting place,

Tended with loving care,

To have parades and ceremonies,

Remembering them and their sacrifices,

To let all of those who survived,

Remember them and celebrate their lives,

For life is fleeting for some,

Long for others,

Memories, heavy in their hearts,

So we should share the load,

And carry the memories forward.

~0~

Remembering Normandy

A trip to Normandy in better times, divine,

Not that day, with advancing the troops,

Saving people in mind,

Beach obstacles, guns,

Pillboxes, razor wire, and mines,

Stood steadfast in soldiers' way,

Rain fell from overcast skies,

Waves unfurled in the bay,

Scattered strong winds,

Blew the paratroopers,

Round and around,

Large waves swamped vessels,

Men struggled to find solid ground,

Artillery was lost,

Still the men did not nestle,

Egos put aside they advanced,

Over obstacles anew,

They gave their all,

Their very lives,

To fight, to gain the ground,

With the air filled with cacophony of sound,

To hasten victory legitimately,

Hard won,

The following year in May the war done,

Five thousand, four hundred, Canadian graves,

Left that day,

Many hearts of families' broken they say,

So long ago, June eighth, nineteen forty-four,

Allied troops deaths added,

Six thousand, six hundred, more,

We remember the sacrifice,

For they fought hard and rolled the dice,

We remember the damage done to them that day,

And honour the memories of those brave souls,

And the valiant actions and deeds,

Of those brave soldiers,

Our need?

To remember them still.

~0~

Section 11 - Pride and Holidays

My Canada

I live in beauty,

A country so wide,

People who care,

For each other,

Is our pride,

When I visit places,

In this country,

So vast and open,

I am thankful,

For freedom to speak,

Freedom to learn,

Freedom to live,

In harmony and joy,

For my country,

Is Canada,

The colour of acceptance,

All creeds, all colours,

All orientations,

We are on under the flag,

Of the maple leaf,

We wear with pride.

~0~

An Ode to our Canadian Hockey Players

T eamwork, working side by side,

Our hockey teams fought hard,

To win a gold,

Together they stood,

Divided they would fall,

Through goals against they advanced,

Stifling opponents, moves precise,

Scoring goal after goal,

They fought hard and won,

Proudly they sing 'Oh Canada',

As we sing loudly along,

Feeling pride for their hard work,

The food and booze flows,

Our parties begin,

But before that we thank,

Or teams women and men,

Thank you for your fair play,

Thank you for representing your country,

Your province, your city,

You are our pride and joy,

Our teams to cheer,

Win or lose.

~0~

Vacation

Vacation is fraught with expectations,

Making plans that come to fruition,

But often reality is different,

As weather, time and circumstances, interferes,

The beach is off as rain and wind comes down,

A sunny day with clouds causes waterspouts,

The geese at the park chase you away,

As does their excrement under your feet,

The drive-in theatre though nocturnal,

With movies you don't want to see,

And unpredicted deluge of rain pouring down,

The summer weather turns cold,

No sweater in the car,

The tendency to whine and cry,

That nothing works out,

The honorable thing?

To embrace the changes and go with the flow,

Or change plans on a dime,

Find excitement, in rain or shine,

Fun found, time with loved ones,

Forever enshrined in lasting memories,

Of laughter and smiles.

~0~

Hallowe' en

Hallowe'en the scaring time,

Where goblin and monster,

Are all seen in sheltered light,

Giving us such a terrible fright,

As they scamper through Hallowe'en,

The witches, the devils, the ghouls,

The kings and the queens, the fools,

The princesses, the fairy godmothers,

As the mist comes and smothers,

The world with its cold tendrils,

The children's laughter trills,

As the children get their fills,

Of candy and chips at our doors,

As the night goes on the lull bores,

We want to get our fright,

From the Hallowe'en night,

From the movies that we see,

Oh, how frightened we can be,

At every little sound,

We liken to fright,

As the children go home,

And the dark hours loam,

And the teens come out,

As they rally and shout,

'Will it be trick or treat?"

"What do you have to eat?"

As the candy dwindles,

And the night spindles,

Coming to an end,

Spiralling into tomorrow,

All Saints Day,

Hallowe'en is gone away,

Our need for chills and fear,

Satiated for now,

We will get our fill,

Come next year,

When Hallowe'en arrives again,

And darkness comes to call.

~0~

Victoria Park

We have a park downtown in London, Ontario, Canada that
they decorate year after year with Christmas lights and
decorations. It is very beautiful and I love to go see it year
after year. It never gets old.

Gleaming lights, snow laden boughs,

Trees aglow, with lights a plenty,

Glittering snow, feathery in its fall,

People smiling, walking on the crunchy snow,

Music loudly played for all to hear,

Christmas carols ring loud and clear,

Joy is in the air and on people's faces,

Memories surround from other places,

It's in the park way downtown,

The place that holds memories,

Of other Christmases long ago,

Victoria Park its beauty behold,

World War II sacrifices commemorated with,

Musical Carillon, eighteen bronze bells,

Singing in the breeze,

Children and adults alike,

Have that gleaming childlike wonder,

Wide eyed, smiles forming on their faces,

As they see the decorations,

Santa's sleigh and the reindeer at play,

Santa's house where Santa can be found,

Each tree aglow with lights,

Then centred near the skating rink,

The manger scene,

The baby Jesus and his family,

Three Kings in attendance,

To bring him his due,

As they look on the winter wonderland,

It makes them think of days of old,

Christmases long past, but not forgotten,

In the minds and hearts of Londoners,

Who celebrate this tradition still.

~0~

Hold onto Christmas

Hold onto Christmas with both hands,

Spread joy and love throughout the lands,

Keep the love within your heart,

Through the year let it never part,

Fill your days with giving,

And maybe even forgiving,

Those who have lost their way,

Most of all find time to smile,

Let sad days and cares float away,

~0~

Christmas Dreams Fulfilled

C hristmas dreams shining so very bright,

Children's face filled with imagined delight,

Visions of stockings filled with goodies and toys,

All good things will come to good girls and boys,

Families imagining being all together,

Grown children who have lost their tether,

Back in the fold for one day at least,

Joined together in love, happiness and feast,

Presents are given, opened and set aside,

For the greatest gift does truly abide,

Within their hearts and in their view,

Memories made, time spent fun ensued,

For family ties have been renewed,

Being together, the greatest gift of all,

Christmas Dreams fulfilled!

~0~

Hanukkah

Hanukkah festival of lights,

Candles burning bright,

Nine-branched Menorah,

One candle each night,

And one extra to light,

The fight they won,

The temple purified,

A miracle performed,

As wicks burned on,

Eight days with oil,

For one long night,

It burnt so bright,

Commemorated each year,

To remember the gift,

Of the single brilliant light,

Burning so long so bright,

Three blessings said,

Three blessings given,

Two each night after,

Giving thanks to the eternal King,

Our lord God is everything,

Happy Hanukkah!!

~0~

Excising Christmas

The tree is down,

The ornaments and cards,

Put away,

For another day,

The presents unwrapped,

Awed over and enjoyed,

The goodies sit on the counter,

Awaiting the garbage can,

While my waistline looks bigger,

No time for tears,

The time for weeping is done,

I put on my exercise clothes,

Bite back my sighs,

And recriminations,

It's time to start again,

To get back the shape,

I once was,

I step on the treadmill,

Only forty miles and,

Forty pounds and,

Three hundred and fifty seven days,

To go,

Before I start again.

~0~

New Year' s

T he bells ring out,

It is New Year's dawning,

It's only midnight,

Yet I'm still yawning,

The cheers ring out,

The smiles bright,

The kisses reign,

On this very night,

As people nod,

Kiss on the lips,

Eat the food,

That goes to the hips,

The wine and drink flow,

Yet I want to go,

I like the company,

But I'm so shy,

I do not like the hugs,

So I sigh,

I do not like the lips,

That find mine,

Soggy, drunken kisses,

I decline,

I smile and nod,

But I want to go,

And still I nod and listen,

To the flow,

Of conversation incoherent,

I fear,

Then I see my husband near,

We talk without words,

As he cocks his head,

And we say goodbye,

Finally off to bed.
~0~

I hope you have enjoyed this book of poetry. Please consider leaving a review at your favourite retailer and please check out my other books at Amazon.
Sincerely S. G. Lee

Please check out my other titles.

PARANORMAL TITLES:
Love's Labour's Won
A Tiger's Heart Wrapped in a Player's Hide
Reborn – a novella~ prequel
MYSTERY
A Penny Saved A Murder Earned
A Diller A Dollar A Really Dead Scholar
Betty Blue Lost Her Holiday Shoe
The Kelly Murder Mysteries-Book 1-3
A Stitch in Time-prequel
Dreams Can Kill
SHORT STORY NOVELLAS
Murder Most Fowl
Jack be Nimble
ObsessionX2
The Stuff of Nightmares
Paranormal
Day of the Dead
Legends, Folktales and other Stories
CHRISTMAS
Christmas is Calling
A Christmas Card
The Christmas Angel
Visions of Sugarplums- all Christmas stories in one

POETRY
A Poetic Touch - The Human Condition

NEWEST MYSTERIES
Stray Bullet~ *the story of a sheriff combatting the murders of his entire staff on his first day and a drug ring selling fentanyl*
Book 4 of the Kelly Murder Mysteries – *What Will Poor Robin Do?*
The Kelly's and the Stewart's have suffered a great loss in losing Carol's parents. Emmett is at odds with Lily as Sherry-Anne and his son is living with him. Carol, Caleb and Rose have joined forces to investigate the accident site and they run into the murderer and are put in peril again.

Please find an excerpt from Stray Bullet and What Will Poor Robin Do, on the next few pages.

Excerpt from Stray Bullet

Preface:

In the small town of Driftwood, Colorado, under starry skies, residents went about their business. The town was now ready for the arrival of the new sheriff having gussied up the urban decay with a few coats of paint. The new sheriff would see the bad parts of town soon enough the mayor thought and turned over in his bed and went to sleep. The hospital looking after a few patients was unusually quiet under the full moon; other people in the settlement getting ready for bed and then turning on late night programs or setting alarms and climbing into bed. Across town a man getting ready for bed after a long hard day at work completed his paperwork, stripped naked and stepped into the shower. As the water ran down in torrents the shower glass doors shattered, the man fell to the floor and rivets of blood ran into the drain. He was the first to die that night.

A few doors over gunman entered killing the husband and wife in their beds and the children as they slept. Blood covered the floor and ceilings in those rooms. None of the neighbours heard a peep they simply slumbered on. Other homes across the town were entered and the residents, husband wife and children were also shot and killed. No one had time to shout out or call 911. It was all over in a few minutes with no time for whimpers only the muzzle of silencers doing their jobs and hitman scurrying into the night.

"It's done, boss. The teams are leaving the state. Yes, I'll do that now. He's coming in the morning. I'll check in after I meet him. His name? All I got is G. Bullet not sure of his first name, it's not on any paperwork. . See you, tomorrow… okay Friday," the man said into his prepaid cell phone and then took out sim card breaking it into pieces. Then he discarded it in a nearby bin at the now decrepit old pulp and paper mill. He had to go to work soon. A new sheriff was coming to town and he wanted to be there to greet him.

~0~

Chapter 1 – Friendship Trumps Bullet

My name is G and I'm on my way to a new life to become a sheriff in a town called Driftwood. Sounds boring, doesn't it. If you'd asked me five year ago I would have told you of course it was; but now this is what I need and my daughter needs…a nice quiet life, in a quiet town, where I could raise my daughter without whispers and rumors. You want to more about that statement? I'll get back to that, but I'm told people will want to know about me a subject I'm not really comfortable talking about.

Asked to describe myself I would say I'm tall over six feet…okay six feet five inches. I am muscular, as I lift weights. I'm not overly muscular, just enough to take down the bad guys. Some people think I look like Tom Selleck in his youth, personally I don't see the resemblance.

G. is a short form for my first name but I don't like
to talk about my real first name. Let's just say my
parents grew up in the happy-go-lucky seventies
and were heavily influenced by the weird names
that people gave their children. What you still won't
give up? You demand that I tell you my first name?
You want to play the guessing game?

My first name is unmentionable I don't talk about it
ever!! My last name is wait for it...Bullet...I know a
clichéd name if you ever heard one. Honestly, it's
my name. It has been mine my whole life.

My last name had raised a few eyebrows. Can you
imagine how many chuckles I've gotten when I tell
anyone my full name? Still can't guess? Some of
you have deducted correctly. So now you know
why I usually don't divulge my first name.

In order for you to understand the relevance of my
last name I'll have to explain more about my family
and their origins.

My grandfather when escaping persecution in
Russia came through at Ellis Island and decided to
Anglicize his name to Bullet; so my dad used that
and now I do.

What's that you like to know grandpa's original name? Well so would I, unfortunately he took that name to his grave leaving no clues behind. But he was great man, a hard working cop. I come from a long line of cops. With a last name like Bullet it tends to earn respect being a cop.

Grandpa was killed on the job by some backward gangsters bent on destroying one another. My dad swore he never be a cop and went to San Francisco were he promptly fell in love with my mother went to the police academy there and then impregnated my mother.

After I turned one he decided he needed family and got a job as a cop in the city where his father had served and brothers now served as cops. When he worked there for six months he had planned to send for mom and me and marry her. Unfortunately the first day on the job he ran into a domestic situation and was killed in the line of duty. He hadn't told his family about my mother or me so we came as a surprise when mother showed up with me in tow for the funeral. They soon adapted however and accepted her and with her me.

When I was four years old, my mother learned she was dying of breast cancer. My dad's three brothers, James, Bennie, and Alfred also cops, stepped up to raise me. They were a demanding bunch always pushing me to be strong and tough. I had to be resilient and learn all the fighting techniques that they taught. Let's just say I am proficient in a number of fighting techniques.

Their younger sister, my Aunt Louisa was a teacher
and just starting her career when they took me in;
however Aunt Louise found plenty of time for me.
She made my childhood more normal though my
uncles would often say she shouldn't coddle me.
My uncles drove her away with their constant
beratement and by the time I was in my teens she
moved to teach in Colorado to save her sanity. She
still managed to chide the uncles into letting me
visit her in Denver in the summer for two months;
the best two months of the year for me.

Getting back to my uncles they hated my first name
as much as I did (though I think they liked me even
less; but did their duty). They also felt that I had
come out of nowhere so they nicknamed me Stray
and it stuck; that's what most of the cops on the
force called me. Aunt Louise was the only one who
ever called me; by my first name.
Why do I speak of my Aunt Louise? Aunt Louise
had recently retired to a small town called
Driftwood Colorado and I often wished she had
been closer especially when I had run into the wall
of blue at my job. Cut to today as I told you earlier
I'd taken a new job as the sheriff in the same town,
Driftwood Colorado.

As I drove to the Sheriff station; I saw that the downtown area was newly painted but other parts were decrepit and rundown. Stores had been closed and signs had been posted that said for rent but the places looked like they hadn't been rented in a long time. The back alleys showed signs, of hookers working their wares with discarded condoms, beer bottles and other paraphernalia.

The town was surrounded by trees; but the main source of jobs in the past had been lumber and the company had pulled up stakes and moved away. Factories and brickyards were closed.
Some of the homes have seen better days and the downtown core was eerily quiet, with vacant storefronts lining the streets. Crime which in the past hadn't been a problem was suddenly up and maybe that's why the Sheriff had quit? But that was the reason I was here. I'd shape this town into a town we could all be proud of again if the re-elected mayor could do as he promised and bring in the jobs. I wanted to be happy here.

I'd just dropped off my three year old daughter with my Aunt Louise. Stella Marie, my daughter seemed okay with the new place and Aunt Louise; but was I? Aunt Louise was sixty years old and a retired school teacher. Why was I so worried? First day jitters obviously. Aunt Louise had my back. She knew what idiots her brothers really were and how they valued their friendships even more than family. Being a single father I needed her more than ever.

Aunt Louise had urged me to apply for the vacant job of Sheriff after hearing about my troubles as a cop in a suburb of Halton, Illinois. I don't want to get into those troubles right now. Today was a new day and I decided it was going to be great even if it killed me. Just kidding! I was not going to get killed like my dad had on the first day of the job. Nerves were getting to me.

Sure it was hard settling into a new place for a child. A little voice worried that I had made a mistake; but this was a new start for both of us we should be happy. A month ago I had been offered my dream job, Sheriff of a small municipality in Driftwood, Colorado. Driftwood looked to me like a small town of three hundred people where I'd be happy raising Stella-Marie.

The streets were tree-lined; the cookie cutter houses had beautiful floral displays out front. The lawns were immaculate green and lush. Children rode their bikes up and down the streets with no fear of predators or gunplay. The people had seemed friendly and warm when I came for my interview for the job. What more could we want? I'd thought.

I'd done my research; but nothing had prepared me for the men all walking out on me. I stepped into the Sheriff's car.

This blue flu wouldn't do! I knew from the dispatcher that the other cops were not happy with my appointment because I was an outside hire; but damn it was my first day on the job and they had a duty to serve and protect the citizens of Driftwood.

How could the four deputies just not show up for the day? Calls to their residences had gone to voice mail so they were even avoiding talking to me. I had to put my foot down hard or the men would never respect my leadership. I'd already faced a wall of blue in my old job; people pulling out the old politics line and drawing in ranks on the thin blue line. I'd wanted a new start to change the harassment I'd faced in my not so fair city over the last three years.

A bit of a long story which we'll get into later but suffice to say the line in blue was put up against me; simply because I stood up to another cop who committed a crime.

Driving down the road to go to my new deputy's home I grew angry. Hadn't I been through enough of this crap from the guys in Halton? I had been harassed day and night by those assholes.

I had to pull myself together; anger would not solve this problem. I could show them I was in charge but approachable. I was an outsider, hired on line. Hell I hadn't even met any of this guys but I would get along with them they just had to give me a chance. No that sound desperate and I wouldn't be that anxious. I would be the best Sheriff and boss they ever had.

Parking the squad car and mounted the wooden steps on the house. I knocked lightly on Deputy Gregory Barnes door. No answer. I gave it my best thundering police knock and the door swung open of its own accord. I pulled my service revolver and entered the residence wily. A smell of dead berries and apples entered my nostrils. I felt in my pocket and then taking it out swished my menthol medicated lip balm under my nose. My adrenaline kicked in and suddenly I felt exhilarated and hyper aware.

I followed the putrid odor to a bedroom and found the late Greg Barnes with two bullet wounds to the heart surrounded by a dried rusty brown pool of blood. He'd been there at least two days. Nothing was disturbed in the home. No overturned furniture, nothing seemed out of place. He lived alone; so no help there. Was it a rogue girlfriend? Why was he dead?

What the hell? The first day on the job and my deputy is murdered? I needed those other cops that hadn't come to work today to help me solve this murder. Damn them and their blue flu.

I made the call to the coroner who was on call for autopsies. Then I secured the scene and called in the neighboring counties police force on loan until I could find my police force.

Less than an hour later, I had two officers, Alfred Jones and Paulo Scarlatti, I sent to the two of them to retrieve the first officer Joseph Paciocco on my list. Imagine my surprise when he called back to tell me that my other officer, Joseph Paciocco was dead too. Two shots to the heart and it looked like the same felon. Was I going to find all my missing officers dead?

A quick search of the other residences found all of the bachelor cops dead shot the same way. The family men with their families at home were dead too; but so were all their family members. They had all been shot with one shot to the head in their beds. They had not stood a chance. This was a professional job as each scene had been carefully scanned and nothing was left to find in the way of evidence other than the blood and bullets.

All in all the dead were Gregory Barnes, Joseph Paciocco, Jack Abrahams, Paul Jones, his brother and fellow officer, Harold Jones and Harold's wife Cheryl, and their two children, Gail, and Fred, Vincent Vecchio and his wife Paula Antrim (both cops on the force), their baby, Adrian a newborn was alive in his crib and was taken into custody of the Children's Aid until a relative could be reached. Also dead were Robert Di Salvio and his wife Rebecca and their fifteen year old son William and their daughter Helen eight years old, Kas Mahmoud his wife Dayita, and their three sons, Aaban, Aahil, and Aatif ages five seven and nine.

What in the hell was going on? Someone had killed whole families. Why? Did they know something someone didn't want them to know? Was it retaliation?

This meant looking into backgrounds and finding out things people didn't want you to know. Being the sheriff didn't make for a popularity contest in any case but this would have to be handled very delicately.

The police officers on loan couldn't continue to investigate this after all I only had a temporary loan of their services for today. Even if I wanted to investigate I had to have help. I needed to call the FBI pronto and I knew just the guy my former partner, Gordon Chum.

I dialed Gordon's number by heart. He answered on the first ring asking me about the new job and then said he'd speak to his boss and get the okay to bring a team down as soon as possible.

Meanwhile I was trying to comfort the staff left at station and ducking calls from reporters from all over the country and residents of Driftwood who were demanding to know what had happened. I took deep soothing breaths…Gordon would be here soon we'd get to the bottom of this. Penny Ambercrombie the office dogsbody and police dispatcher took charge and hustled the troops off to their stations to work on the tasks I'd given them. Penny was tall and lean possibly one hundred and ten pounds though it was hard to tell for her clothes hung on her in non-descript browns that did nothing to enhance her looks and she stood at least six feet tall. Her hair was a rich chestnut and was wound tightly at the nap of her neck into a bun. Her eyes were her most striking feature that not even her terrible clothes sense could hide as they were a glittering emerald green that showed immense interest and intelligence. She appeared to be in her late twenties though her skin was leathered with the weathering an outdoors enthusiast had.

I could see that Penny was be an asset to me and the sheriff's station in my job. But first I needed to call Aunt Louise and Stella- Marie and hope my daughter wouldn't get too upset that daddy would not see her until tomorrow at the earliest.

I picked up the phone and called the number by heart. There was no answer. Where could she be I wondered? My question was answered in the next few seconds by my office door swinging open. There my Aunt Louise stood with Stella Marie. Aunt Louise demanded, "Gunner is it true? Are they all dead?"

The next thing that happened was three year old Stella-Marie jumping in my arms and saying "Daddy, I missed you."

I closed my office door no sense in putting on a show to the remaining troops and I hoped no one had heard my aunt utter my first name. Stella-Marie took the chair nearest me.

"I want an answer Gunner."
"Not in front of the c.h.i.l.d."
"Ch. i.ld, child, that's me," my precocious daughter answered.
"Stella-Marie already knows all about this. She turned on the television while I was in the bathroom and she heard about all your deputies and their families being found dead. She insisted I bring her here."
"Then you both know what I know. I'm investigating and I've called in the FBI."
"Daddy, are you safe? In that movie with the Kung Fu guy they tried to kill him and then killed his family," Stella-Marie answered.
"What have you been watching?"
"I remember his name, now. I love Jean Claude van Damme movies," Stella-Marie stated.

"Me too, pumpkin and we're safe. I haven't been here long enough to be mixed up in whatever is going on here," I reassured.

"You'll find the bad guys?"

"Daddy will find them. That's what daddy used to do before he had you," I answered.

"Be careful," Stella-Marie said with adult wisdom beyond her years.

"Stella-Marie is correct. You need to stay safe."

"I promise both of you, I will stay safe."

"We'll trust you."

"Can we have dinner together, daddy?"

"Of course we can my apple dumpling."

"I'm not an apple dumpling."

"No you're my little pumpkin."

"You're silly, daddy."

"What would you like for dinner? Pizza? Chinese food?"

"Pizza! I want pizza!!"Stella-Marie chimed.

I ordered her favourite Hawaiian pizza and we forgot work for a few minutes as we ate. Stella-Marie told me about her day between bites. Stella-Marie sounded happy and was adjusting well to living in this new place. She didn't seem too worried about my job anymore. She kissed me goodbye and said, "Get'em, daddy. See you tomorrow, nighty, night."

I breathed a sigh of relief my daughter seemed happy despite all that was happening. I was the new sheriff so the danger to me from who ever committed these murders must be minimal if any, so my family was safe. Still I told Aunt Louise to keep Stella-Marie indoors and keep the doors locked reporting any suspicious activity to me.

Gordon arrived a few minutes later, "I'm Special
Agent Gordon Chum FBI," he said showing his
badge then continuing he said, "I'm here to take
over this case."
"No. You're not you're here to assist me and the
good people of Driftwood."
"I am here to serve the people yes, and if that means
taking over the investigation in a town that has seen
fit to kill all its police officers save one..."
"How dare you? This town is peaceable. There is a
perpetrator or perpetrators who have committed a
heinous crime but we will get to the bottom of this."
"You should have recused yourself Sheriff."
I heard Penny Ambercrombie gasp and then mutter
under her breath, "What a maniacal idiot and a kook
to boot."
"No, shouldn't! This was my first day on the job. I
was to begin tomorrow but I thought I'd get in and
do a little paperwork first. I am imminently
qualified to investigate this. I hadn't even met these
men or their families; but I care very much about
what has happened to them. They are police officers
and my squad. Every one of them is mine so this
crime was committed against me and my family. Do
you understand?"
"I understand the feeling and I promise not to step
on your toes, Sheriff. My men and I are at your
disposal in this investigation. You are in charge.
Perhaps we could discuss the particulars before my
colleagues get here?" Gordon stated.
"Please follow me this way to my office, Special
Agent Chum," I answered.
"Call me Gordon," my pal offered.
"People call me Stray, or G," I stated.

Gordon pretended to be shocked and lifted an eyebrow at me. Penny looked at Gordon with disgust but went back to the front desk of the station.

Gordon entered my office and shut the door, loudly. Spotting the pizza he said, "That went well."
"Yes, it did. Did you see the dispatcher, Penny Abercrombie craning her head and her ears to listen to you?"
"I saw her when I came into the station. She was frowning at you and giving you dirty looks when you weren't looking like she didn't believe you belonged here, Gee."
"I noticed those looks all day," I answered.
"That should be the end of that you can thank me now. She is directing those looks to me now and I'll wager she'll spread all over town how you defended the honor of the dead."
"Thanks Gordon for the assist; but how will we can we keep up the lie?"
"We begin a new friendship," Gordon said calmly then continued, "I hope you saved me a few slices of that pizza, I'm starved and my team is checking into the No-Tell Motel down the street within the hour."

I smiled and nodded handing him a couple of slices. It was good to see my old partner again.

"You are staying with me and Aunt Louise aren't you?" I asked.

"Lucky for you or is it me they are limited space in this town to stay and of course this allows me to begin a new friendship with you. All my agents have taken up the last rooms in the motel so I'm grateful your aunt will put me up. You did ask her didn't you?"

"Didn't think I had to, you know Aunt Louise loves you."

Gordon raised another eyebrow.

"Fine I'll call her now."

I dialed and Aunt Louise answered her cell phone on the first ring. Aunt Louise said of course Gordon was staying here. I told her not to tell anyone we knew her and she agreed after I told her why. Then she said she had to go as she had pulled over to answer the cell phone.

"So it's settled?" Gordon asked.

I nodded.

"What a terrible first day on the job for you pal," Gordon commented, "Especially after what happened to you more than three and half years ago."

I thought back to what I had been through the last three and half years and I found myself reliving that chaotic time in my mind.

I'd been about eight years on the job in the city of Halton, Illinois, a cop, just like my dad and grandfather and uncles before me. The city had gone to the gangs. . It was two steps and one step forward. Every time we turned around; another shooting another victim of a drive-by. Just the other day the victim was a seven year old kid innocently riding their bike! Luckily the kid lived; but we actively hunted for the shooter or shooters. I should have took that as an omen seeing as my grandfather and my dad lost their lives in the police service, but I went merrily on my way doing my job not expecting my life to come crumbling all around me.

A routine call to a richer neighborhood for a disturbance started it all. The dispatcher didn't think to tell me it was a domestic disturbance and the man had a gun. I'm always careful in those situations; more careful then the average cop but if you don't know you can't take precautions.
I knocked on the door and announced myself and shots barreled through the front door grazing my forehead and tearing my knee apart. I burst through the door grabbed the shooter and he shot me again. That should have got me accolades and medals right? After all I was shot doing my job, but no, all of those rightly went to my partner, Gordon Chum. The third shot resulted in a thigh wound that almost made me bleed out on the spot if it wasn't for the quick work of my partner Gordon Chum securing the prisoner and belting my thigh. Okay, so I got a medal or two, but Gordon was the real hero. See why he was the first man I called when my force had been gunned down.

Gordon is a second generation Asian American. A good looking fellow and kinder than most men, he speaks softly and carries a big stick. People underestimating him rather walk away unscathed. Gordon standing at five foot six weighed roughly two hundred and ten pounds of pure muscle. He knew every fight technique I knew and more. He saved my life a time or two.

Gordon was arguably one of the best partners I've ever had. Gordon saved my life after I was shot on duty and secured the scene until back-up could get there. He also called for an ambulance for me. I was carted off to a hospital where I spent the next three weeks in intensive car being prayed over by my fellow cops, and the rest of the city.

Whatever chits they called in with the big guy upstairs it worked, I survived and I should have been happy about that; but all I could think was I missed my moment I was supposed to die like my dad and my grandfather before me on the job. It wasn't that I was that different when I came out of the coma. Okay, so I had a few scars inside and out. My forehead now sported a scar that I could cover with bangs and temporarily bum leg. The leg didn't seem to want heal in fact at one point they threatened to take off my leg; but good old Gordon helped me fight them on that and the knee healed to the point I could walk on it. But it wasn't good enough for work, at least not then.

Suffering from self-loathing (and yes a little post-traumatic stress disorder, if I truly admit it); I began to be curt with everyone closing myself off from everyone and everything. My wife, Gina took the brunt of all of this. I was cruel to her at every turn. When she came to visit I'd ignore her.

I knew I needed help from the police shrink but I couldn't accept or admit that I, the wonder boy actually had a problem. Gordon begged me to quit loathing myself so much and making everyone else around me miserable but I didn't listen. I was content to wallow in my anger and self-loathing. Weeks went by and Gina seemed unhappy despite her forced saccharine with me. She gave me an ultimatum get help; or she would leave me. I decided I wanted Gina so I found a shrink of my own choosing Doctor Collins for his add in the Yellow Pages.

Doctor Collins turned out to be a woman.
Don't get me wrong she wasn't a fantasy (that blonde fantasy with legs up to here and hiding behind glasses); no she was more like your grandmother. Non-descript, her silver hair short and curled tight to her head. Her voice was soft and she always offered me milk and cookies before a session. I kind of felt weird at first like she was family and I'd never been all that chatty with family anyway. I had so much trouble talking at first that I'd just sit there and stare at the walls; but after a few sessions she got me to open up about my childhood and then finally about the shooting. I began to feel better and worked on getting my knee back in shape so I could return to work.

I had a routine and I followed it. Therapy followed by afternoon sessions of psychotherapy. With the drugs Doctor Collins prescribed and all our talks I began to almost feel normal again. Okay, so I'm lying; I still had a few stray thoughts that I was a failure and that I should have died; but I labored hard to overcome them and worked on being nicer to my ball and chain. I even began to buy her flowers. As for my leg it was almost good enough to return to work.

Doctor Collins had scheduled my appointment for two p.m. on a Friday and I had looked forward to getting it over with and going home to surprise Gina. A cop buddy had offered me his family cottage and I planned a trip to the Poconos for the next week. I'd already called Gina's work and got her the next week off. It would be a fantastic surprise for her and a chance for us to just lay back and enjoy our weekend. I could even cook all the meals that I caught from the lake as it was loaded with fish.

I decided to change my appointment and let Gina know that it would now be at noon instead of two p.m... Surely I could charm my shrink into seeing me earlier and if not well then I see her next week after my trip. I arrived at the doctor's office to find a note on the door. It seemed my shrink. Doctor Teresa Collins had died suddenly this morning and they were rescheduling. A number to call followed the announcement.

Died! And all they thought about was their schedule? Devastating and only then realizing how close I had gotten with my shrink I fell to the floor crying and took about a half- an -hour to recover enough just to pull myself together. I told myself over and over everything would be okay but I didn't really believe it.

Enough of this shit!! A little therapy and I turned into a wimp; who cried at the drop of a hat. I was a Bullet and we were strong manly types; made of steel not mush!! People died!! Get over yourself I admonished myself. I had a life... a wife who loved me despite myself. It was time to man up and be the husband she deserved. I just had to get away with Gina. I'd go home and surprise her now.
Stopping at the gas station to fill-up and walking into pay I spotted roses. I picked some up and thought how pleased Gina would be. She deserved this after all I'd put her through the last two months. She'd surprised me two weeks ago, telling me that she was pregnant. I was overjoyed looking forward to our baby coming in six months.
We had a new beginning and I would make her as happy as Gina had made me.

I thought about the look on her face; her joy at our baby and decided to book her favourite restaurant before we left town. We could then leave at nine p.m. I'd drive all night and we reach there by morning. It could be done despite my gimpy leg. Okay so I lied, I wasn't fully recovered; but soon I would be. My physical therapist was pleased and said I might even be able to go back to work in a month.

I went home opening the front door with my key and... You know what happened? It was that other old cliché...husband comes home and finds his wife naked doing the tango with another naked man.

I didn't recognize him from the back as he jumped out the window, naked clothes in hand. She could tell me who he was in her own good time. And I had plenty of time as I seethed and wanted to kill him but not her. I didn't want to hurt her at all I just wanted to take her in my arms and make this go away.

I took huge breaths and then realized it takes two to tango. I had brought this on with neglect and coolness towards her when all she did was support and love me. I took deep breaths to calm myself and rationalized. I was sure this was just a one-time thing.

I'd heard women could get quite horny in pregnancy I obviously had let her down.
I had been a terrible husband moody brooding, distant and angry. Gina deserved better and I could forgive her this. Couldn't I? Sure I was angry, but I would never harm Gina despite my thinking for her lapse in judgement. I had stared at her five foot nine naked figure with its well-endowed breasts and tiny waist and wondered how she hid our baby in it.

Her curly black hair fell in ringlets to her waist. I realized I loved her. I loved our baby. It had been my neglect that had driven her to this; I was prepared to forgive her and take her on my planned trip. We'd been married fifteen glorious years, okay so not glorious, fiery; but she was also pregnant and I wanted my child to have a stable home with two parents one of them me. I'd been spared so my kid could grow up with a dad it was as simple as that.

I told Gina all of this and she laughed. It seems that she and her paramour had been carrying on since day one of one of our marriage. Once more she had an amniocentesis last week and received the results this morning the baby was his not mine. I was devastated all those dreams of playing catch with my daughter. Taking her to daughter and daddy dances. Having her look up to me, with hero worship came crashing down. Yes, I know it could have been a boy; but I had my heart set on a girl. I admit it I went against all my principles and begged her to stay and claim the baby was mine. We were married so the baby was legally mine. She laughed that twinkly laugh that I knew so well and I had to restrain myself from retaliating as she told me she already left me I just hadn't noticed. Gina said she was tired of living a lie. Now that I knew it was all out in the open and she file for divorce and move in with him. She lunged at me slapping me and asked why could I be like him?

I want to hit back at her but I couldn't if I it back I wouldn't be any better than the men I arrested who abused their wives.

Why couldn't I be like him? The man that she slept
with, she raged. I was stupefied and getting angrier
by the moment I knew I needed to leave before I
regretted losing my temper; but I needed to know
who had replaced me.

She laughed again and said I find out soon. I begged
her to tell me and she did.

HIM?

I fell to my knees. How could it be him? No, it
wasn't Gordon Chum; but someone else I
considered a friend and brother. Gordon wouldn't
do that to me. The dirty dog who had betrayed me
had been a partner, a mentor and good grief the man
was old...fifty five if he was a day and close to
retirement.
Why had she cheated on me with my former partner
Derek? He'd broken the cop code you didn't sleep
with another cop's wife. He'd slept around I heard
how many women he'd been with had she? I told
her and she laughed telling me it was his cover
story. She continued snickering and said at least
every woman didn't try to pick him up in front of
her. She packed her bags and then trounced out the
front door to join him at his house.

I thought I could handle it all and maybe I could
have if she hadn't come back a half an hour later
saying she'd changed her mind. She stripped to her
skivvies and begged me to change her mind. What's
a hot blooded male to do? I wanted to prove I was
the better man, the better lover, so I turned my back
and began stripping too.

That's the last thing I remember before waking up in hospital. How I got there and what happened after that I couldn't recall until much later.

The doctor kept speaking to me but it sounded like gibberish. My brain didn't want to understand. I don't know why. I closed my eyes, but before I drift under I hear them talking.

"Will he be okay now, doctor?" Gina asked. "We'll know better when he answers my questions," I perceive the doctor say far away.

I recalled hearing footsteps as someone left. A voice I recognized as Gina whispered in my ear, "You stupid son of a bitch. Why didn't you die? You'll wish you had now."

I struggled to wake before she could harm me; but I remember it was like moving under quicksand. I heard an alarm sound and footsteps run into the room.

"What did you do you now, you evil bitch?" I heard Gordon yell as I feel myself falling through layers of unconsciousness into nothingness.

0~

If you'd like to read more of this book go to **http://authl.it/8sk** *to purchase this book in paperback or kindle.*

Excerpt from What Will Poor Robin
Do?

Chapter 1 - Bleak New Year' s

Cold and raw the north wind doth blow,
Bleak in the morning early,
All the hills are covered with snow,
And winters now come fairly.
Wind doth blow and we shall have snow,
And what will poor robin do then, poor thing?
He'll sit in a barn and keep himself warm,
And hide his head under his wing, poor thing.
~Old Nursery Rhyme-Author Unknown

The day after Katha's wedding at the Airport

"Such a lovely wedding, you and Grandpa Terrence looked so wonderful yesterday. What a party! You danced into the night; while I watched you both twirl and boogie the night away. Grandpa Terrence can really dance. I think he put all of those younger guys to shame."

"He's really fit. The doctor says he's like someone twenty years younger," Katha answered.
"I think I had about three hours sleep," Lily stated.
"I told you to go up to bed, three times," protested Katha.

Katha then looked at the peaked Lily. Lily's face was drawn and worn looking and her hair hung limp and scraggily around her face.

"Are you sure you're okay?" Katha asked.
"I'm fine. I had my personal physician sit with me most of the night until I went up to my room," Lily laughed.
"Dafydd is pretty cute. Terrence is his godfather and says he was always a good kid."
"Yes, he is nice," Lily commented then a frown came over her face as she thought about how she met him and what Emmett had done.
"Do you want to talk about Emmett?" Katha asked.
"No! Can we change the subject?"
"You should see all the pictures I took," Amelia stated overhearing, "I'm taking them in so you can have a nice album of physical pictures, Aunt Katha."
"Physical pictures?" Katha asked.
"Adults over forty should come with manuals," Rose muttered under her breath then closed her eyes and went to sleep.
"I'll take the pictures off my phone and in the camera and transfer them to a disc; where I'll take them to a photo place and they'll develop them to pictures you can put in your album or on the wall," Amelia explained.

"That should make a nice album, along with the ones the photographer took," Katha cried, happily looking at the pictures on Amelia's camera.

"I'm glad you like them," Amelia said.

"Ooh, could I have a copy of this one? I'd like to blow it up and put it on our wall," Katha exclaimed.

"I can get that done at the photo place along with the others. What size do you want of you and Terrence dancing?"

"Oh that is a good one! You look younger than your years!" Lily commented looking over at the photo, she then yawned.

"I'd like an eight by ten," Katha stated.

Terrence then came back from the men's room and asked, "Eight by ten what?"

"Picture dear for our wall don't we look good in this picture?" Katha asked.

"We do," Terrence agreed.

"I'm going to take a nap until the flights called. Wake me up when our flight is called will you Grandma Katha?" Lily said.

"Me, too," Amelia said yawning.

"I will. Now go to sleep, my sweets," Katha answered then turning to Terrence she said, "A magical wedding, wasn't it, Terrence? A castle all my family and the man of my dreams; what more could a bride want?"

"I'm so glad that I married you Katha O'Malley," Terrence stated taking her in his arms and kissing her soundly on the mouth.

"That's Katha O'Malley- Stewart; thank you," Katha replied.

"Look at the children and they say youth has more energy. Rose and Carol are sound asleep, too," Terrence answered.

"They do look so sweet."

"It was a fun trip for them too despite the unpleasantness. Wasn't it?" Terrence enquired.

"Yes, darling, I think they had a good time, although something is up with Lily. I believe something more than breaking up happened to her and Emmett. She's not saying anything to me, though," Katha stated.

"Lily seemed fine to me. Are you sure?"

"Lily thinks she's hiding her hurt from me, but I see it. Something happened."

"Will you pry it out of Lily?"

"No, I'll wait and then get the whole story out of Amelia in about a week's time. Lily always confides in her cousin; or Lily will tell me in her own good time."

"You really love your girls. Are you sure they'll be okay if we take our week's honeymoon in Paris."

"What?"

Terrence showed Katha the airline tickets that said London Ontario to Toronto to Paris. Katha couldn't help it she squealed happily like a little girl, "We're going to Paris!!"

"Your girls are headed home to Happy Valley. I already told Lily and their flight leaves before ours."

"Oh, Terrence you spoil me. I haven't been to Paris since I was with... I'm sorry; I'm with you now I shouldn't bring up one of my other husbands," Katha stated.

"We both have a past, my darling girl. It's what's brought us to this true love. I understand you love Kieran, too. That's what made us what we are today the sums of our pasts, but I'm the lucky one I have you by my side. "

"No wonder I love you. You have a heart as big as an ocean."

"I have to if only to match you my darling, Katha."

Katha then glanced at the tickets again.

"Don't worry Grandma Katha. I booked the tickets and triple checked them. You're really going to Paris," Rose stated looking up at them with sleepy eyes.

"You're awake? Will you girls be okay if we go away?" asked Katha.

"We'll be fine, Grandma Katha. Rose, Carol, Amelia, and I will see you two when you get home; until then have fun," Lily exclaimed opening an eye and commenting.

"You included me as one of Grandma Katha's girls?" Carol puzzled.

"Why wouldn't I? You were always unofficial family before but now you're now officially family."

"Thanks, Mrs. Brooksfield," Carol answered her voice choking up.

"I'm your Aunt Lily now."

"Thanks, Aunt Lily. I'm tired too, somebody wake me up when they call our flight to Happy Valley," Carol said.

~0~

Francine and Gerald Banks

Francine glanced over at Gerald with love.

They had both celebrated this New Year's Eve; Gerald a little more than Francine. He'd given up the keys willingly; smiling that smile that melted her knees. Gerald looked over at Francine and smiled a goofy smile and Francine felt deliriously happy. She wanted to shout to the world that she and Gerald had reconciled.
Her girlfriends had told her she had lost her mind for forgiving and forgetting his indiscretions which had caused their break-up, but Francine had loved Gerald since she was a teen and that had never gone away. She needed him in her life and by her side.

Francine covered a yawn with her hand. Her head ached and she was tired; a little sugar would pick her up; one of those orange custard squares Daddy had given her would taste great right now. A little pick me up to get them home at four a.m. on New Year's Eve. Francine smiled again at Gerald and he touched her arm.

"I love you Francine, you are the best thing, which ever happened to me," Gerald claimed "I'll never cheat on you again."
"You'd better not. Or you can bet I'll take you to the cleaners with that pre-nup my lawyer drew up. I hope that's not just the champagne talking."
"It isn't. I promise we'll be a family again and Carol will be happy. You'll be happy too. I will really try harder this time, Francine."

"Just don't hurt us again, Gerald."

"Here, I'll prove my love to you. You were thinking about those lemon squares your Dad gave us; weren't you? Sometimes I think you love sweets, more than me."

"You do know me, and I love you more than life itself, Gerald," laughed Francine as Gerald held a square up to her mouth, eating another square himself with his other hand.

Francine made short work of the square not even tasting it, she ate it so fast. Coconut fell into her lap and with one hand she brushed it off taking her eyes off the road for a moment.

"Oh no Gera....aa...ld it has ginger in it!" cried Francine.

Francine grabbed her throat with one hand and tried to pull over before she passed out. Gerald tried to take the wheel, but in his excitement, the square he ate choked him and he seized his throat with frantic motions.

Francine passed out, her breathing laboured and then almost non-existent, Gerald too, his breath laboured as he can't even eke out a cough and tries to reach again for the wheel. Their car skidded into the path of a tractor trailer. The car, a mass of twisted metal hit a guard rail. It wound between trees and through grass and down an embankment.

Gerald choked up the square too late and died. Francine stirred for a moment between life and death and prayed, silently, "Dear Lord, I accept that it is my time; but please grant me one last goodbye to my daughter and find someone that will care for her as I would."

~0~

Carol

Carol snuggled deeper into the airport chair hearing Terrence and Katha talk some more she stopped listening. She'd sleep until their flight was called. Three a.m. was an ungodly time to get up. It felt like she'd been up for eight hours and it was only nine a.m. Carol closed her eyes surrendering to the deep REM cycle of sleep, something however interrupted this. Carol felt herself stirring to a wakeful state and then felt her mother's hand touch her brow. Carol then struggled to open her eyes.

"Carol, honey wake up." Francine begged.
"Mom, I don't want to get up. I'm tired I want to sleep."
"Baby, please listen I don't have much time. I want to tell you how much I love you."
"Love you too, mom. Want to sleep now!" cried Carol keeping her eyes closely closed.
"Your dad and I both love you and we were together when we died," Francine began.
"What do you mean you died? I don't understand Mom? I think I want to wake up now. This dream is weird!" Carol cried opening her eyes.

Carol looked at her mother and saw that a mist surrounded her and there was a see through quality to her. What a strange dream.

"Why do you look like that?" Carol asked puzzled.

"It's a long story Carol and time is short. I want you to listen to me now, baby girl. You were the best thing in my life in besides your Dad. Being your mother? Truly a gift and a blessing; remember that!"

"I don't understand Mother .Why do you tell me this?"

"There's no easy way to say this, Carol. I'm dead baby! I'm so sorry to leave you. I choked on ginger and the car crashed. Your father and I are dead. I know you are terrified. This will be a trial for you my little love, but don't you will survive this. Rose will be by your side and she understands. Go to Rose, share with her and let her in. Your Grandpa Terrence will take care of you it's in our will."

Carol watched as Francine turned around quickly as a bright shiny light appeared. An outstretched hand reached for Francine pulling her close. Carol realized she knew that hand-it was Grandpa Crimshaw. Were they all dead? Mom said that she and Dad were dead. If Grandpa Crimshaw was dead too, how did he die? She wanted to wake up, now!!Then all this would go away but as she came fully awake and saw the airport again she could shake the feeling that nothing would change. This wasn't a dream at all; but a goodbye. It had to be… it had seemed so real. No, she was borrowing trouble as Grandma Katha said. Wasn't she?

Carol felt the tears coming down her face. She questioned the dreams purpose for a few seconds, trying to convince herself again that it was a dream; some convoluted dream conjured from her overtired mind.

However it felt real; not like a dream but like an interactive video recording. She looked around the airport as if she could see their manifestations. Grandpa had been mean and miserly. If he had died she should feel some grief for his passing; but all she could think was why he couldn't have just died and her mother and father live.

Carol looked around begging for someone to tell her the dream wasn't a premonition, or her mother hadn't really appeared to Carol after death. Carol felt numb inside; like someone had turned on air conditioning in the airport, an impossibility in winter. Now she knew what they meant when they said chilled to the bone. Carol looked over at Rose slumbering on. Rose must have felt this way when her father died and yet Carol hadn't really understood.

Carol felt bad; but she didn't feel this pain down to her very marrow, not about Rose's dad.

Carol heard her cell phone ring and ignored it. Looking to the caller she saw it was Great-Uncle Edward she didn't want to answer. She knew what he would say. She didn't want to hear it, if no one said it, it wasn't true!

"Well, hello, Edward," Terrence answered as his phone rang seconds later, "I'm sorry you weren't able to get away for our wedding. It was wonderful everyone had fun. …What? Say that again… No, that can't be possible! That can't be true."

Terrence face appeared ashen and in that moment he looked like he had aged twenty years.

"Terrence, what has happened? Tell me!" Katha demanded, worried.
Terrence couldn't seem to form words; so Carol took a big breath and said calmly, "My Mom and Dad are dead and so is my Grandfather Crimshaw."

Terrence didn't dispute what Carol said, tears coming from Carol's eyes.

"How do you know that Carol? Are you psychic?" asked Rose.
"My mom told me," Carol answered.
"But if your mom is dead how could she....?"

Lily stared at Rose hard and then Rose exclaimed, "Carol, I can't believe this. I am so sorry. Whatever you need I'm here."
"I'm so sorry, my darling grandchild. I loved Francine with all my heart. I'd like to believe my granddaughter did come to you in your hour of need. We are all here for you, Carol," Terrence said sadly wiping away tears.
"That's right, we'll cancel our honeymoon. You come first," Katha volunteered.
Terrence nodded and said, "Excuse me, a moment. I have to change our tickets to Happy Valley."

Terrence then went directly to the counter to change the tickets.

"This is real?" Carol asked, then resigned she sighed and said, "Yes, of course it is. I wanted it to be a horrible nightmare but it's awaking one. "

"Carol; I'm so sorry. Remember you have your family and we are with you now," Terrence said.

"Terrence is right. You are our great-granddaughter and we all love you. We are here for you, always," Katha stated.

"We love you, Carol. We are your family and here for you," Amelia stated.

"Come here, Carol," Lily insisted, as she wrapped her in her arms, "Amelia's correct; we are your family, Carol. Don't forget that. We grieve with you. I am so dreadfully sorry about your mother. I know how much it hurts to lose your mother; but each individual is different and I would never compare myself to you. I also understand that your pain is your own; but if you ever want to talk about anything I'm here for you."

"Thank-you all, I just want to think about them right now. It just seems so unreal, like I'm in a mist," Carol admitted.

"It will get better dear. I know it doesn't seem so; but it will," Katha advised.

"It will never be better," Carol answered then began crying.

Lily held onto Carol tight and let her cry; soon Carol wiped her tears and sat stoically waiting for the flight. Others in the airport looked on in sympathy and that made Carol feel even worse. She soon dried her tears when their flight was called. The staff, solicitous allowed them to board first. Terrence, Katha, Amelia, Lily, Carol and Rose all board the plane with heavy hearts. They all thought of Carol as the plane took off and they flew home.

Terrence stared to wonder if Francine suffered. The Kelly ladies wonder if the curse of the Kelly's had touched Terrence and Carol's family and if this is the price people paid for loving them.

The plane landed and they find the press waiting for them shouting questions at them, "Do you know anyone who would want to murder your family members?" and "Is there any connection to the murder of the mayor months ago?" followed by "Is your family cursed?"

Terrence steered them through stating, *"No comment."* to the press. Terrence then hustled them out of the airport to Katha and Terrence's home. They were home, time to face the music. The honeymoon was over before it began.

~0~

Happy Valley

Ding dong, the asshole's dead. He lorded over everyone. People thought Harold Crimshaw had won fairly over Katha O'Malley; but they were mistaken. Harold Crimshaw had rigged the election in his favour. He deserved to die; there was no doubt about it. Not that Katha O' Malley would have been a better mayor; but at least she was honest.

Harold Crimshaw was evil incarnate. If no one would do anything about such man well then I had to do something. I couldn't allow him to continue to use his position and power to harm anyone else. Harold nattered on about how you should go do what you loved best while destroying lives. So inspiration struck me. Harold loved oranges, so oranges should kill Harold with a little help from ginger. So me, the murderer (tee-hee-hee, love that term murderer.) took his life with what he loved most oranges.

Filling his ample gut with the sweet squares I made with my own two hands. It was really too bad that his daughter and son-in-law were killed; but they really shouldn't have been so greedy. The squares were made so lovingly for Harold. His daughter was his spawn so she probably had those evil genes anyway and as for the son-in law he could have been picked by Harold. I'd heard he was a cheat and a terrible father. So no great loss and yet I felt a measure of guilt.

It wasn't my fault they ate them and that she had inherited Harold's unusual allergy. I mean really who's allergic to ginger? Harold that's who! Except now he wasn't allergic to anything anymore; except maybe the cold hard ground.

I still had to dispose of the evidence. It must not get in the hands of the police. The evidence would implicate me. If they found the squares...I must get the container the squares were in. I must get there to Harold's house and get access, but how? Where there's a will; there's a way. I knew of a way and I would take it. Harold was dead and he wouldn't harm anyone again and that was the way it would to stay. I would see to that.

The police really weren't looking at this as a crime. They think it was death by misadventure. Ha, ha, they think it's an allergy gone wrong. No crime involved; maybe I'm in the clear?

Barbara Franks was in charge at the Crown Attorney's office. Lily Kelly Wentworth-Brooksfield had stuck her nose in the wrong place on holiday and now was on sick leave. Something about her heart? You stick your heart in the wrong place and it get twisted Lily should have learned that a long time ago.

Timing was everything; Lily Kelly-Wentworth-Brooksfield was such a nosy broad. She wouldn't have let this go and then I would have had to do something to her.
Lily was such a lovely person too; so that would have really hurt to have to take action against her. She was even sweet to Barbara when Barbara was suffering her depression so bad that she lashed out at Lily. It really helped that Barbara was a stickler for the book; everything by the book no deviations. Barbara would close the case in no time. Despite the fact that when I committed this crime I didn't know the police chief Edward Stewart was related to that idiot Harold it wouldn't harm me. It wouldn't bring me down. I allowed myself a sigh of relief. Then I analyzed the problem. It wasn't my fault his stupid granddaughter ate what was meant for Harold and ended up killing herself and her husband. I mean really could I have predicted that? Should I have?

Edward Stewart was no fool. I must not underestimate him and his zeal to find me. The silly man wouldn't shut up about how someone had killed his great-niece. Funny thing, he wasn't complaining that much about Harold. I guess he didn't like him much either. Too bad, about the kid though, being an orphan was a tough gig. I feel bad about Carol Banks.

No kid should lose their parents so young, but then again it really wasn't my fault her mother was so greedy and killed them both and she was better off without her stupid cheating low-life father.

My plan was in action I had rid the world of a dirty politician, a pervert of the worst kind, a thug. So why was I feeling guilty? He chose his death not me!!

He had the choice to eat, or not eat the orange squares and he had chosen. I mustn't lose my focus I had to keep an eye on the investigation discreetly. No one must guess I was behind this. Blame got me nowhere. I must protect myself at all costs.

Barbara Franks was in charge at the Crown Attorney's office. Lily Kelly Wentworth-Brooksfield had stuck her nose in the wrong place on holiday and now was on sick leave. Something about her heart? You stick your heart in the wrong place and you get it twisted. Lily should have learned that a long time ago.

Timing was everything; Lily Kelly-Wentworth-Brooksfield was such a nosy broad. She wouldn't have let this go and then I would have had to do something to her. Lily was such a lovely person too; so that would have really hurt to have to take action against her. She was even sweet to Barbara when Barbara was suffering her depression so bad that she lashed out at Lily. It really helped that Barbara was a stickler for the book, everything by the book no deviations.

Barbara would close the case in no time; despite the fact that when I committed this crime I didn't know the police chief Edward Stewart was related to that idiot Harold. That wouldn't bring me down. I allowed myself a sigh of relief. Then I analyzed the problem. It wasn't my fault his stupid granddaughter ate what was meant for Harold and ended up killing herself and her husband. I mean really could I have predicted that? Should I have?

Edward Stewart was no fool. I must not underestimate him and his zeal to find me. The silly man wouldn't shut up about how someone had killed his great-niece. Funny thing, he wasn't complaining that much about Harold. I guess he didn't like him much either. Too bad, about the kid though, being an orphan was a tough gig. I feel bad about Carol Banks. No kid should lose their parents so young, but then again it really wasn't my fault her mother was so greedy and killed them both and she was better off without her stupid cheating low-life father.

My plan was in action I had rid the world of a dirty politician, a pervert of the worst kind, a thug. So why was I feeling guilty? He chose his death not me. He had the choice to eat, or not eat the orange squares and he had chosen. I mustn't lose my focus I had to keep an eye on the investigation discreetly no one must guess I was behind this. Blame got me nowhere. I must protect myself at all costs. Barbara Franks was helping me and didn't even know it. Soon she'd close the case and that would be the end of it. It would all be over. Wouldn't it? Of course, it would.

They'd never find me. I would always be that illusive murderer that none of them knew about. Too delicious!! I was a success at last. Take that daddy!!

~0~

If you'd like to purchase What Will Poor Robin Do? , in kindle, or paperback, go to http://authl.it/8sn.

S. G. Lee

www.ingramcontent.com/pod-product-compliance
Lightning Source LLC
Chambersburg PA
CBHW051939090426
42741CB00008B/1198